OVERTON COUNTY, TENNESSEE

Genealogical Records

Compiled by
EDYTHE RUCKER WHITLEY

CLEARFIELD

Reprinted for
Clearfield Company, Inc. by
Genealogical Publishing Co., Inc.
Baltimore, Maryland
1997, 2002

Originally published as part of the series
entitled *Tennessee Genealogical Records,*
Nashville, 1967
Reprinted: Genealogical Publishing Co., Inc.
Baltimore, 1979, 1983

Library of Congress Catalogue Card Number 79-50040
International Standard Book Number 0-8063-0841-9
Made in the United States of America

CONTENTS

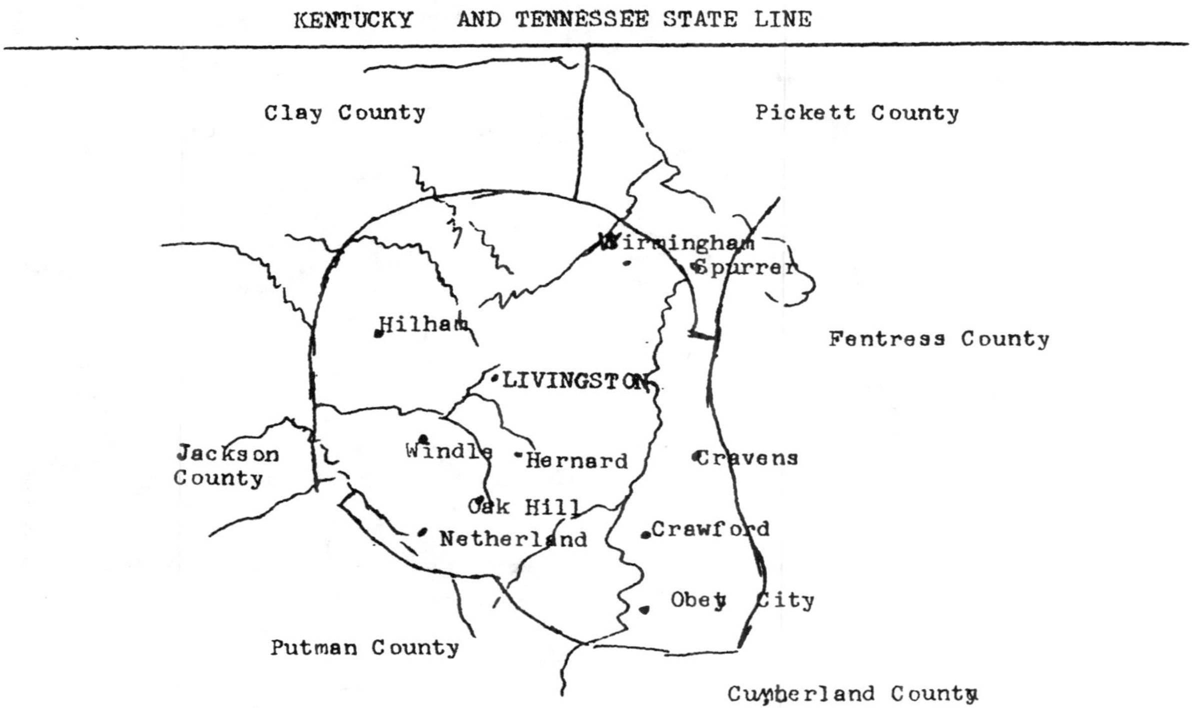

The above map of Overton County, Tennessee shows the general lay of the county and town locations

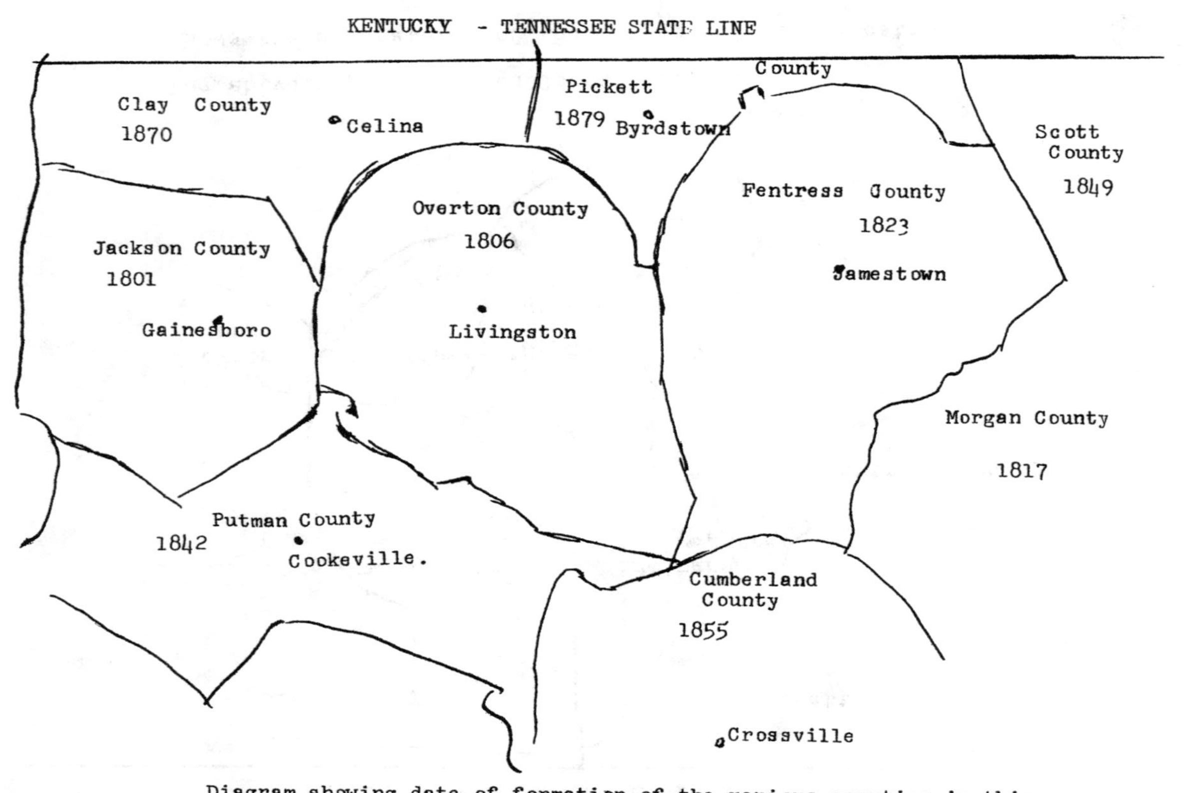

Diagram showing date of formation of the various counties in this section of Tennessee.

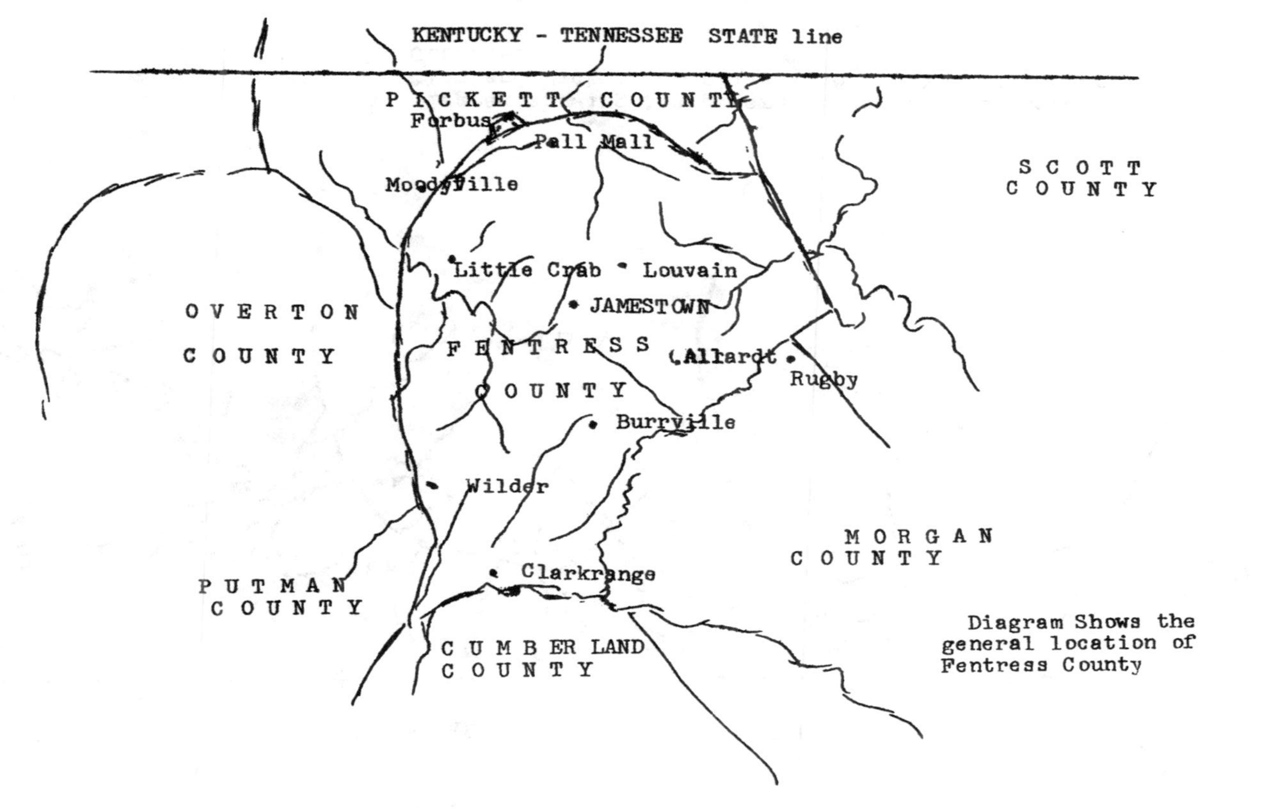
KENTUCKY - TENNESSEE STATE line
PICKETT COUNTY
Forbus
Pall Mall
Moodyville
SCOTT COUNTY
Little Crab
Louvain
JAMESTOWN
OVERTON COUNTY
FENTRESS COUNTY
Allardt
Rugby
Burrville
Wilder
MORGAN COUNTY
Clarkrange
PUTMAN COUNTY
CUMBER LAND COUNTY
Diagram Shows the general location of Fentress County

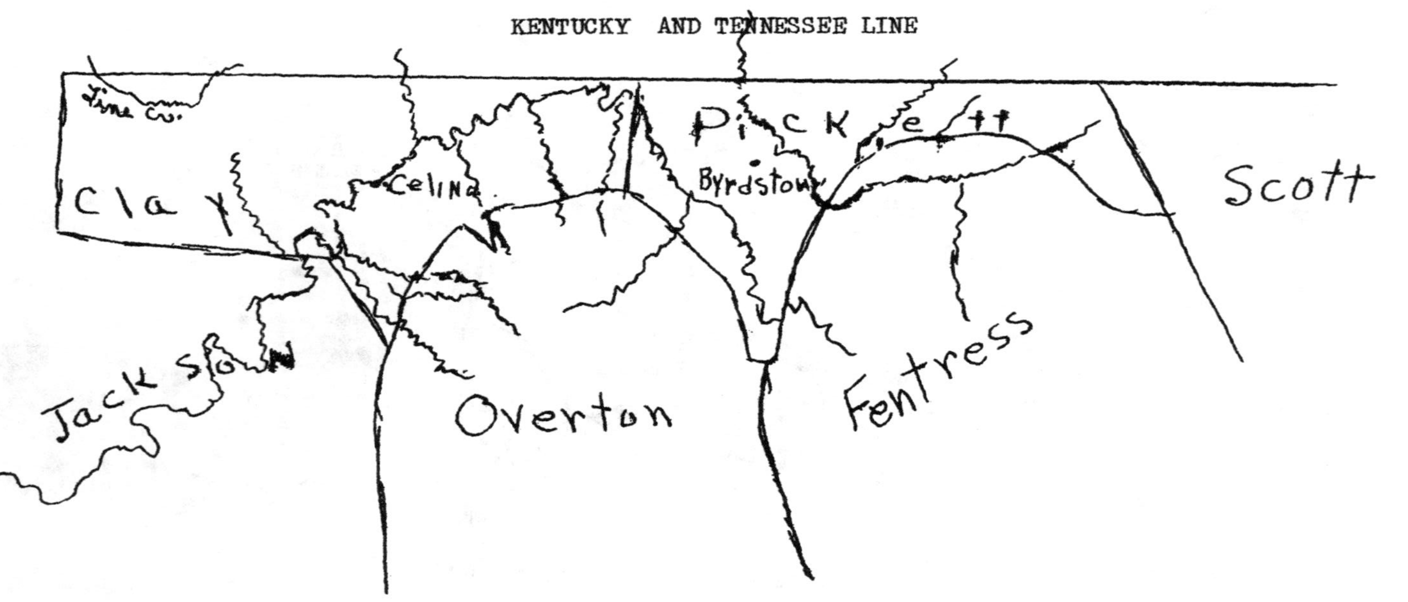

Diagram showing the general location and shape of Clay and Pickett Counties with Overton and Fentress Counties.

Genealogical Records

INTRODUCTION

In order to write intelligently about Overton County, Tennessee,it is necessary to include some of the vital facts about her children -- Clay, Fentress, Pickett and Putman Counties.

Overton County is one of vital importance since it once included either all or portions of Fentress, Clay, Pickett, and Putman Counties. At the time that Tennessee was admitted into the Union, 1796, most of the wilderness, now known as the Upper Cumberland Country, was a part of Sumner County, becoming a part of the New County of Smith in 1799, and a part of Jackson in 1801. Overton and White Counties were both established in 1806. No further changes were made in that area for several years.

Overton County was named in honor of Judge John Overton, the most intimate friend of President Andrew Jackson. The boundary was described as extending from the Kentucky line to the Wilderness Road leading from Walton's Ferry and from the top of the Cumberland Mountain westward to a North and South line striking Kentucky at the point where the Cumberland River enters Tennessee.

There seems to be a question as to the exact place of the first court of the new county. Some authorities claim it was held at a place called Jones' Store, about five miles north of Livingston, while others claim it was held at the house of Benjamin Totten at Monroe. Reference is made to the latter location in Deed Book A, Page 190, of the Overton County Records. It is possible that Totten resided at or near Jones' Store, and both statements are correct. It is, however, a well known fact that great rivalry existed between that place and the town of Livingston five miles north of the first location. It was not actually settled until an election which was held in 1833, Livingston being victorious by a small majority. Monroe was the first county seat, with a population of 200 people. It was so designated by an act of the General Assembly passed June 1, 1810.

It was at Monroe that the home of Joanne Goade Sevie Windle stood, and near which place is her grave and those of her son and his wife. Joanne Goade Sevier Windle was the daughter of Governor John Sevier, who had received vast acre of land in that section by grants.

The oldest town in the County is Hilham, founded in 1806 by Moses Fisk. It was here that the Fisk Female Academ was located, the first school distinctly for girls charterec in the South, and one of the first in the United States. The school was founded in 1803 by Moses Fisk and in 1806 was chartered by the Legislature of the State of Tennessee. The Female Academy existed only about two years, but many peopl came to the home of Mr. Fisk to be taught. Fisk was educated at Dartmouth College and Yale University. He came to Tennessee in 1796, first locating in Knoxville. He came in possession to large tracts of land which is now Overton, Clay, Putman and White Counties.

Overton County's main waterways are Obed and Roaring Rivers, tributaries of the Cumberland River. The surface of the country is hilly, and its soil very fertile. It excells in being excellent cattle and sheep lands. It has some of the finest timber lands in the country.

In the present day it is known for the fine recreation facilities afforded at Dale Hollow Lake, and may be termed "Sportsman's Paradise".

In 1802 the total population of Overton County was approximately 1030 families.

Joseph Copeland is said to have been one of the first three settlers in what is now Overton County, and became a friend and associate of Nettle Carrier, the chief of the Indians who resided here when the white people began their settlement in this section.

On the mountains above the head of Nettle Carrier Creek was a village of the Cherokee Indians. The site of the village is now known as the "Indian Graves". In this village were two young braves who were in love with the same Indian maiden. To decide who should marry her, they went to the Chief of the tribe. The old Chief told them to each throw a sprig of green into the waters of a nearby creek, and that the one whose sprig was carried the farthest by the water should marry the girl. One threw a nettle, and the other a thorn. The nettle floated farthest, so this thrower married the Indian maiden, and from that day was called Nettle Carrier. The creek which carried the nettle was named for him, and bears the name Nettle Carrier. Afterwards the community took the same name, and was so called by the early white settlers.

This lucky Indian became chief of his tribe, and many white people a few generations ago became his neighbors. Nettle Carrier was the last Indian chief to reside in this section, and tradition has it that he lived here until 1799.

David Crockett was born in 1786. He lived in that part of Overton County which became Fentress. Deed Records show that he was here in February and in September, 1817. His home was above eight miles West of Jamestown on the East Fork of Obed's River. It stood on the brow of the hill below the cemetery on a place later owned by Harve Smith. The spot is now marked by stones that once formed a part of the chimney of Crockett's cabin. He is supposed to have been related to the Travises, the Beatys and other Crocketts in the same section.

Others among the early settlers were Colonel Stephen Copeland; and his son "Big Joe" Copeland; John Goodpasture; Capt. Jesse Arnold; Capt. Simeon Hinds (the father of Dr. J. I. D. Hinds of Lebanon, Tennessee); Benjamin Totten (the father of Judge A. W. O. Totten); Judge Alvin Cullom; and Adam Huntsman.

I am not attempting to write the political or economic history of Overton County, but wish to acquaint my readers and the student of genealogical research something of the general information needed to carry out their study.

In 1850 to 1860 the postoffices and postmasters in Overton County were: Fox Spring, with Jonathan C. Sewell as postmaster; Hilham, with Thomas J. Murphey as postmaster; Livingston, with Andrew J. Goodbur, Postmaster; Locust Shade, with John M. Turner as postmaster; Mill Creek, John Rose, Postmaster; Monroe, A. M. Garrett, Postmaster; Netherland, Richard Poteet, Postmaster; Nettle Carrier, Rawlings H. Johnson, Postmaster; Oak Hill, Quin M. Gardenhire, Postmaster; Olympus, Abram Grimsley, Postmaster; Walnut Grove, James M. Goodbar, Postmaster; and West Fork, with Abraham Gearhart as Postmaster.

By Chapter 302, Public Acts of Tennessee, creating Fentress County, passed at Murfreesboro, November 28, 1823, Jonathan Douglas was appointed to survey the boundary lines of Overton so as to reduce it to its Constitutional limits of 625 square miles. Jonathan Douglas was the son of William Douglas, and a brother of Henry Douglas who was killed by the Mexicans at Giliad in 1836.

By Chapter 327, Acts of 1825, Isaac Taylor was appointed to resurvey the lines of Overton County beginning at the Johnson Stand, "the southeast corner of said County."

At the same time Overton gave up a portion of her territory for the creation of Fentress County, Morgan County also was required by an act of the Legislature to relinquish a portion of her territory which was included in the new county of Fentress.

Thus Fentress County was created in 1823, and was named in honor of the Speaker of the House of Representatives, James Fentress, who served five consecutive terms, 1814-1823. The County seat was then at a place called Sand Springs, but later changed to Jamestown, which name it retains until this day.

In 1827, John M. Clemens, the father of Samuel Clemens (Mark Twain) was a lawyer residing in Jamestown, and

Obedstown of the "Gilded Age" was the Jamestown of that time, more familiarly known as Jimtown.

The first court was held at Three Forks of the Wolf's River. The first Courthouse was built in 1828, and Jamestown was incorporated in 1837. It is said that the plan for this courthouse was made by Mark Twain's father, who was the first Circuit Court Clerk of Fentress County and by far the largest landowner. It is also said that he was the Si Hawkins of the "Gilded Age."

Obey's River, or Obed River, is said to have been named for one of the long hunters, Obadiah Terrill. The county is drained by Obed, Clear Fork and Wolf Rivers, and Clear Creek, a tributary of the Tennessee River.

This county was the home of the notorious Federal bushwhacker "Tinker Dave" Beattie, and of Calvin Longston who, with others, perpetrated cruel and bloody deeds in reconstruction times; and also of Marsha Millsaps who, in 1843, was charged with being a witch; and of "Old Man" Stout who, in 1835, was accused of practicing witchcraft.

The records in the County of Fentress being destroyed by fire in 1904 make it difficult to determine who the early county officials were. Mr. A. H. Hogue in "One Hundred Years in the Cumberland Mountains" refers to several collections of old papers, and gives some scattered names and dates of their various offices held.

Among the first settlers of Fentress County, while it was still a part of Overton and Morgan Counties, were: Conrad Pile, Pearson Miller, Arthur Frogge, John Riley and Moses Poor.

This county in late years was the home of the famous Sergeant Alvin C. York, whose wonderful exploit in World War I, is familiar to everybody. Your author well recalls the ovation, which she attended in Nashville, on the arrival of the hero, fresh from the battlefield of Europe.

In 1850 and to 1860 the postoffices in Fentress County were: Boatland, with Solomon Alberton as Postmaster; Coopersville, with Pemberton Gatewood as Postmaster; Hale's Mills, with Jonathan D. Hale as Postmaster; Jamestown, with John P. Martin as Postmaster; Pall Mall, with Henry Gatewood as Postmaster; and Travesville, with Charles B. Ryan as Postmaster.

In 1924 the postoffices in Fentress County were: Allardt, Alticrest, Armathwaite, Banner Springs, Ben Stockton, Boatland, Brown Place, Clarkrange, Coonrod, Davidson, Forbus, Gernt, Grimsley, Helena, Jamestown, Manson, Mount Helen, Pall Mall, Riverton, Roslin, Shirley and Wilder.

On February 1, 1842, Putman County was erected by an Act of the State Legislature from parts of White, Overton, Jackson, Smith, and DeKalb Counties, and was named in honor of General Israel Putman of the Revolutionary War.

White Plains was named as the place where all courts should be held until a permanent site could be established for the new county. This was the farm of S. D. Burton, three and a half miles east of Cookeville. The commissioners appointed to carry out the act were: Isaac Buck, Burton Marchbanks, H. D. Marchbanks, Richard F. Cooke, Henry L. McDaniel, Carr Terry, Elijah Carr, Lawson Clark and Grover Maddux. The Act provided that Mounce Gore , well-known surveyor of Jackson County, should survey and make a plot of the new county site.

For half a century previous to the erection of Putman County, its territory was largely included in the bounds of White, Jackson and Overton -- the three counties cornering on a large chestnut tree, on the north side of Walton Road at White Plains.

In accordance with the provisions of the act creating this county, the county and circuit courts were established and their officers were elected and functioned until 1844 when an injunction restraining the officers from performing their duties of their offices was applied for and granted. February 11, 1854, however, Putman County was re-established largely through the efforts of Major Richard F. Cooke, after whom Cookeville, the county seat, was named. He was one of the most prominent citizens of the county, and at the time was an influential member of the State Senate. The Commissioners named in the re-organization act located the county seat and laid off the town which was named Cookeville. The land for the town of Cookeville was purchased from Charles Crook, who made the deed to the chairman of the County Court, Robert D. Allison, and same was recorded on Page 219, Book A, in the office of the County Registrar and is dated 2 July 1855. This is one of the few record books to escape the courthouse fire of several years ago. Major Richard F. Cooke was a native of Culpepper County, Virginia, born January 8, 1787. He grew up in Greenville District, South Carolina, and emigrated to Maury County, Tennessee, in 1810 and two years later opened up the farm known recently as the Thomas Holman place three miles from Double Springs, on the Gainesboro-Sparta road. Major Cooke was an officer in Woolfork's Battalion under General Andrew Jackson in the War of 1812. He was twice a member of the State Senate. He died October 15, 1870.

The commission named in the re-organization act was composed of Joshua R. Stone and Dr. Green H. Baker of White County; Austin Morgan and Major John Brown of Jackson County; William Davis and Isaiah Warthon of Overton County; William B. Stokes and Bird S. Rhea of DeKalb County; Benjamin A.

Vaden and Nathan Ward of Smith County.

Monterey on top of a mountain (called in the early days Standing Stone) and Bloomington Springs are noted summer resorts.

The establishment of a town by name Monticello took place about the time of the re-organization, and the commissioners of the new town were duly empowered to sell lots in the proposed town, and with the proceeds establish a fund to be used in the purchase of land and the erection of public buildings. This was proposed to be the new county seat. The members of this commission were James Bartlett, William H. Vance, John Bohannon, Edward Anderson and James Jackson. After a long delay the commission finally, in 1844, decided upon a location about a mile east of the present town of Cookeville -- the Buck College site -- but this place and their plans were never to mature.

The same year a suit was instituted in the Chancery Court of Overton County seeking to enjoin William H. Carr, clerk of the Circuit Court, and Joseph A. Ray, Clerk of the County Court, from the exercise of their official duties. The court sustained this contention and held that the New County of Putman had been illegally and unconstitutionally established. This chaotic condition existed for some ten years.

Putman County is watered by Caney Fork and the Cumberland River.

Putman County furnished many gallant officers in the War Between the States. Among them were: Sidney S. Stanton, John B. Vance, Holland Denton, Walton Smith, S. H. McDearmon, John H. Quarles, W. B. Carten, S. J. Johnson, Rison Robinson, C. J. Davis, S. G. Slaughter, William Ensor, and Abraham Hord.

Harvey H. Dillard who raised the first Company of infantry to go from this county wrote an extended article for Lindsay's "Military Annals of Tennessee". Page 335 says, "The company I led out, known as the 'Highlanders', was from Putman County, organized in May and mustered into service at Camp Trousdale, 9th of June, 1861. I helped to form the Sixteenth Tennessee Infantry, and constituted the extreme left of the regiment, and was lettered as Co. K; H. H. Dillard, Captain; W. K. Sadler, First Lieutenant; H. Denton, Second Lieutenant; and R. A. Young, Third Lieutenant; with John H. Savage, Colonel.

Then there was General Alvin C. Gillen, one of the three general officers furnished the Union Army from Tennessee, who was from Putman County.

There were only three postoffices in Putman County

in 1856/57; namely -- Bear Creek, with Robert Peek as Postmaster; Cookeville, with Curtis Mills as Postmaster; and Falling Water, with Jack Chilcut as Postmaster.

In 1924, there were ten postoffices in the county; namely -- Algood, Baxter, Bloomington Springs, Brotherton, Buffalo Valley, Cookeville, Double Springs, Monterey and Silver Point.

Overton, along with her neighbor Jackson County, surrendered a portion of their territory to create a new county on December 7, 1870, which was given the name of Clay in honor of Henry Clay.

Celina was selected for the county seat over Butler's Landing and Bennett's Ferry, both of which were courting the hopes of being the seat of justice. Celina is located at the mouth of Obed River, and for many years was the most important trading and shipping point on the Upper Cumberland.

Clay County borders on Kentucky. This county is drained by the Cumberland River and its tributaries, the most important being the Obed River. The surface of Clay County is hilly and the soil very fertile.

In that part of Clay County taken from Overton County, and also in Overton County as it is today, John Sevier located 57,000 acres of land on the visit to which he refers in his diary, a copy of which was secured by the Tennessee Historical Society some years back. After his death in 1815, his widow moved to the Dale, known later as the Clark Place in Clay County. From there she moved to Alabama.

In 1924 there were five postoffices in Clay County, namely -- Celina, Lillydale, Willow Grove, Hermitage Springs, and Moss.

One of the landmarks of Clay County, now more than one hundred and sixty years old is Rock Springs Church of Christ at the little town of Rock Springs, Tennessee. The Church was organized January 1805 and has lived continuously ever since; and is possibly the oldest, and certainly one of the oldest, Churches of Christ in America. The church is located in the Pea Ridge section of Clay County, eight miles northeast of Celina, just three miles from the Kentucky line, and in the rugged hills overlooking from the north that section of Obed River which is now Dale Hollow Lake. It's membership through the years has been maintained at well over 100. The initial service took place in the little log home of John McAdams. It was here they met for some fifteen years. About 1820 the first church building was erected which stood about forty-five years when a new building was erected.

The earliest records of the church are said to be lost in a fire several years ago. The present records are said to date back prior to the War Between the States. Alexander Campbell, "founder of the Church of Christ", "Raccoon" John Smith, Isaac T. Denton, John Newton Mulkey, and many others of bygone days preached here (Nashville Tennessean, Jany. 1, 1949, Gordon Turner).

In 1879 Overton and Fentress Counties gave up a portion of their territory for the creation of a new county to be named Pickett. It was named in honor of H. L. Pickett, who was a resident of Wilson County.

This county is well-watered by Obed and Wolf Rivers. Some of the finest timber in Tennessee comes from Pickett County.

Its early history is the history of the counties from which it was taken. Due to the courthouse burning, there are practically no records of Pickett County, of bygone days.

The Gunnels, one of the best known families in the county, came from Virginia before the county was established.

In 1937 when Cordell Hull, Pickett's County's most distinguished son, was the wise statesman directing the United States in its course of turbulent international affairs, his native county could boast of one telephone and one Negro family in the entire county.

"Pickett County had to put on the breaks to keep from being pushed across the Kentucky line by its parents, Overton and Fentress; with its 'twin-in-age' Chester, it shares the title of the youngest county in Tennessee. And the people who live here declare that when the state had created Pickett in 1879, it was such masterful workmanship that it rested from its 'Acts of Creation' and called this the capstone." (J. Percy Priest, Nashville Tennessean, October 8, 1937)

In 1924 Pickett County had six postoffices -- namely, Byrdstown, Gunter, Oakgrove, Chanute, Moodyville, and Spurrier.

(References: Goodspeed's _History of Tennessee_, 1886
Tennessee Counties, by A. P. Foster
History of Putman County, by Walter S. McClain
One Hundred Years in the Cumberland Mountains, by A. R. Hogue, 1933
History of Overton County, by Judge J. D. Goodpasture
Gleanings from unpublished records, etc.

OVERTON COUNTY, WILLS, DEEDS, MINUTES, ETC.

NOTE: Since the records of Fentress, Pickett, Putman and Jackson are either all or partly destroyed, the records which have not been destroyed for Overton County are of vital importance to the genealogist or historian. The early Overton County books contain a bit of everything. There is no Will Book 1870 in Overton County. The early marriages are not recorded in a marriage book, but scattered through the deeds and minutes, or have been lost completely. There are wills also found scattered through the deed books for the years prior to 1870. The marriage book begins about 1865.

* * * * * * * * *

Deed Book V, Page 2. We, Stephen D. Upton and Matilda Upton his wife have bargained and sold and do convey for and in consideration of the sum of $770 to said Stephen D. Upton paid to Mary Padgett and Lavinia Padgett and their heirs and assigns forever, for a tract of land in Overton County, Civil District No.9, on waters of Little Hurricane Creek containing 250 acres. The same tract of land on which we the said Stephen D. Upton and Matilda Upton now lives, and being the same tract of land once owned by H. P. Hoover and sold by said Hoover to W. E. Upton except 50 acres sold to L. W. Hoover off of the southwest end of the tract on the which 50 acres Said L. W. Hoover now lives. Said 250 acres bound by lands of H. P. Hoover and Adam Deck or claimed by them on the east by the lands of Laben Philip and adjoining land known as the Manning lands and said 50 acres on which L. W. Hoover lives. The tract that was decreed by the Livingston Chancery Court at the January term 1875 in the case of L. W. Hoover VS Wm. E. Upton and others and S. D. Upton, against L. W. Hoover and others and fully described in said cause. We agree to defend title to Mary Padgett and Lavinia Padgett. 3 Feby 1875. Signed Stephen D. Upton and Matilda Upton.

Deeds V, Page 310. I, A. Crawford have this day bargained and sold and transfer to Johnathan Padgett and heirs for consideration of $100 paid, a tract of land in Overton County in Civil District No.8, on Cumberland Mountain, the 100 acres the NW corner of a 5000 acre survey in name of John Barksdale runs south cross the Philip branch, etc . 18 August, 1877. Signed A. Crawford.

Overton County Marriages, 1867-1879, Page 207. Andrew Padget and Miss Eleaner Ramsey, issued Oct.9, 1876, married October 12, 1876. J. A. Allred, J. P.

Overton County Marriages, 1867-79, Page 178. Wm. Langford to Elizabeth Padget, October 11, 1875. married October 3,

1878. A. W. Narred, J. P.

Overton County Marriages 1867-79, Page 176. John Padget and Miss M. E. Tudor, Issued 9 August, 1875, married on 12 August 1875. A. W. Narrod, J. P.

Deeds L, Page 423. March 17, 1851. Indenture William Padgett to Wesley Sells, both of Overton County. 100 acres land sold to Sells by Padgett. Land on waters of Obed River District No.11 runs to Livingston Spring branch to mouth of Osburn Spring Branch, with Livingston line to Archiland (looks like Oxendines) SE corner. Signed by William (x) Padgett, no witnesses. Proved in Overton County, 7 April 1851. W. H. Turner, clerk.

Deeds G, Page 12. Know all men by these presents, John McIver of Fairfax County, and Commonwealth of Virginia are bound to Reuben Padgett of Overton County, Tennessee, for $200, for 175 acres of land held by grant No. 289 lying on north side of Obed's River in the Danlson Cove Tract (Donelson Cove Tract), 3 Feby 1817. Within the bounds of 40,000 acre tract in said Overton County distinguished by the name "DONELSON COVE TRACT" corner of James Howard's tract. It is understood that Reuben Padgett is to pay taxes both State and direct on said land. Land bought on installment notes. $1.50 per acre value. Signed John McIver. Witnessed by John Thurman, Herin Hervery. It adjoins land the widow Pyburn now lives on, and not to interfere with her land. October court 1832. Fentress County, this was acknowledged and proved by witnesses. John H. Richardson, clerk of Fentress County Court. Seems McIver sold 145 acres in the deed originally and then in his lifetime promised Reuben Padgett 25 acres more. Oct.1, 1832. John McClellan. Two bonds of conveyances and probates thereof attached were registered and certified on 14 day Nov. 1834 from John McIver and Reuben Padgett. Signed John Kennedy, Register.

Deeds L, Page 424. Thomas H. Hill sells and conveys to Benjamin Flowers Sr, and heirs forever, for $80. paid a tract of land in District No.11. Overton County, containing 80 acres, on the road leading from Monroe to Monticello then west to the Eagle Creek Road. 7 April 1851. Signed Thomas H. Hill. Witnesses - R. I. Windle. H. R. Craven.

Deeds L, Page 106. Indenture 20 Sept. 1851. Henry Johnson, executor, of John Chilton, deceased, late of Haywood County, Tennessee, to James Flowers and Reuben Felkins of Overton County, Tennessee. John Chilton in his lifetime on 7 July 1838 sold Flowers & Felkins as per his title that date, a tract of land in Overton County on Wolf River, near the road leading across Wolf River at Dillons, adjoining Anthony Flowers. The consideration being $320 in life of Chilton and $180 to be paid. Contained 300 acres. Johnson conveys the land to Flowers and Felkins. Signed Henry Johnson, executor of John Chilton decd. Proved in Haywood County, Tennessee, also recorded in Overton County.

Deeds E, Page 146. Anthony Flowers sold and delivered to Thomas Hill, a Negro woman named Fanny. Consideration $375. paid. 13 Dec. 1820. Signed Anthony Flowers. Test - Willis Huddleston.

Deeds E, Page 72. Indenture 9 April 1796. Henry Flowers, merchant, in Bertie County, North Carolina, to Reverend Charles Pettigrew, of the County and State aforesaid. Henry Flowers for and in consideration of sum of 200 pounds. Henry Flowers conveys sells to Rev. Charles Pettigrew 800 acres land in Sumner County in the ceded "Territory South of the Ohio River", late a part of the State of North Carolina, situated on both sides of the East fork of Roaring River adjoining John Gatlins Corner. Being a part of a patent granted to Henry Flowers of 1000 acres dated 20 May 1793. No. 2131. Signed Henry Flury. Test. Hy Hardy. H. Murphy. Payment of 200 pounds April 9 1796. Copied from Bertie Co. N. C. Registers office.

Deeds E, Page 31. John Barham of Madison County, Alabama, appoints friend Sampson Williams, of Jackson County, Tennessee, my attorney to recover a tract of land in my name in Overton County, Tennessee, joining the town of Monroe, Overton County, said tract of land was conveyed by John McDonald to Thomas Overton and myself jointly 6 Nov. 1818 and same day Overton relinquished his right to his son John H. Overton. Attorney now is to divide said land equally between Overton and myself. 12 May 1819. Signed John Barham.

Deeds E, Page 346. April 19, 1823. Stephen Copeland to the members of "Roaring River Society of Baptist of Overton County", for consideration of $16.00 paid said Stephen Copeland. Conveys 3 acres 40 poles in Overton County, near head of a small spring.

Deeds E, Page 263. 13 August, 1794. Henry Flewry of Bertie County, N. C. to John Gatling of Sumner County, District of Mero, South of the River Ohio, for consideration of 50 lbs, Carolina currency, 200 acres land etc.

Marriage Book B 1867-1879. (Book A is missing.) Page 110 S. H. Flowers and Miss Margaret Smith, Issued July 16, 1870, married by James Conne, J. P.

Marriages 1867-79, Page 191. J. M. Flowers to Susan E. Farrell, issued 17 Sept. 1876 married on the 17th, W. P. Thompkins J. P.

Marriages 1867-79, Page 219. S. W. Flowers to Samantha A. Hill, issued January 9, 1877 married by J. L. Easterly J. P.

Marriages 1867-79, Page 244. F. M. Flowers to M. E. Pierce, January 2,1881, by Isaac Stailey, J. P.

Marriages 1867-79, Page 207. Andrew Padget and Miss Elender Ramsey, Issued Oct. 9, 1876 married Oct. 12, 1876. by J. A. Allred, J. P.

Marriages 1867-79,Page 176. Elijah Garrett and Sarah Flowers. Issued Sept. 30, 1875. married by W. B. Tomkins, J. P.

Marriages 1867-79, Page 269. Haden Garrett to E. C. Flowers. March 6, 1879. by W. H. Parris J. P.

Marriages 1867-79, Page 178. Wm. Langford to Elizabeth Padget, Oct. 11, 1875. married Oct. 3, 1878. by A. W. Norrad J. P.

Deeds V, Page 410. Samuel M. Flowers and Francis Flowers his wife. Samuel M. Flowers being heirs of Samuel M. Flowers, Senr., decd., for $50. paid sold and convey all our undivided interest in a tract of land in District No. 13, Overton County. Polly Flowers his widow now resides on said land. Conveys our interest in said tract of land it being one fourth of said Polly Flowers, except one half acre including the graveyard, Signed S. M. Flowers. Frances (x) Flowers. They acknowledged the above in Hancock County, Kentucky.

Deeds N, Page 443. Jacob Cargile and Susy Jane his wife, and Angelina Flowers, bargain sell transfer and convey to Rolin Flowers and heirs forever for consideration of $165, our undivided interest in two tracts of land in Overton County District No.12 being the land that James Flowers died seized and possessed of containing by estimation 300 acres on waters of Wolf River and bounded etc. On Anthony Flowers line on an old Livingston road, north of road to Wiley Huddleston's and with his line to Joel M. Felkins line to with his line to Eliza Nelens, thence to Reuben Felkins line to James Mullins to line of Anthony Flowers, to Livingston road on Rolen Storys line with line of Zachary and to Hales line. 29 December 1856. Signed by Jacob (X) Cargile. Angelina (X) Flowers. Susyane (X) Cargile. Witnesses - Rolin (X) Story. Joseph Beckham.

Deeds N, Page 366. David Flowers of Overton County, conveys 91½ acres of land on waters of Wolf River in Overton County, to Samuel M. Flowers, Jany 1, 1856 for consideration of $70. paid and acknowledged. Land adjoining Jesse Hull and James D. Jones. Also adjoins Southgate and the widow Riley. Signed David (X) Flowers. Witnesses, Abram Jones. Robert B. Jones.

Deeds N, Page 367. 23 March 1846 Indenture Jesse Sewell of Cumberland County, Kentucky, to David Flowers of Overton County, Tennessee, 91½ acres land lying on waters of Wolf

River in Overton County.

Deeds N, Page 434. Indenture 22 July 1854. Anthony Flowers of Overton County, Tennessee, to Samuel Flowers for consideration of $150. paid. Land in District of No.12. 54 acres on waters of Wolf River in Overton County, the remainder of 74 acres tract conveyed to said Anthony Flowers by Joseph Crawford which deed Book B page 257-8-9. 20 acres of the 74 acres tract is sold and conveyed to Judith Flowers by said Anthony. Signed Anthony (X) Flowers. Test - Rolen (X) Story. Rolen Flowers.

Deeds N, Page 435. Indenture 21 July 1850. Anthony Flowers of Overton County to Judith Ann Flowers his daughter of said County, 20 acres on waters of Wolf River. District No.12, in Overton County. Consideration $60.00 paid. Land in Overton and Fentress Counties on waters of Wolf River and being part of Anthony Flowers 74 acres of land.

Deeds G, Page 214. Indenture 14 January 1836. John and Henry Graham of Overton County to James Flowers. Field Huddleston purchased from our late father John Graham decd a tract of land 10 Feb. 1820, and said Huddleston set over to James Flowers all title. John and Henry Graham confirm to James Flowers all claim etc.

Deeds G, Page 292. Indenture 27 August 1836. John Chilton of Haywood County, Tennessee, to James Flowers of Overton County for consideration $21. paid; John Chilton conveys to James Flowers a tract of land in Overton County on waters of Wolf River. Land Adjoins Scott's corner. To corner of tract of land owned by Anthony Flowers and adjoining also James Mullins. Signed John Chilton. Witnesses James (x) Flowers and William Chilton.

Deeds G, Page 293. Indenture 26 August 1836. William Chilton Senr, and James Flowers both of Overton County, for consideration $35.00 paid convey to Flowers a tract of land in said county on Wolf River on west side said Wolf River to corner of Anthony Flowers tract. Signed Wm. Chilton, Witnessed by James (X) Mullins. Wm. Chilton.

Deeds M, Page 174. Know all men by these presents. Levi Flowers and Ursula his wife in the County of Fentress and Wm. Flowers of the County of Cumberland, Kentucky in consideration of the sum of ______ paid to us by Rolin Flowers in the County of Overton and same acknowledged. Grant, Bargain sell and convey to Rolin Flowers his heirs our undivided portion of a tract of land with all the priviledges and appurtenances to the same belonging situated in District No.12 in Overton County on waters of Wolf River and bounded as follows. Beginning on a white oak on Anthony Flowers line on the Main Road leading from Livingston Tennessee to Monticello, Kentucky, thence northwardly with said road to Willy Huddleston's line thence with said road to line to L. Felkins line, A. Flowers line to R. Felkins line to Mullins line. Our undivided shears in a tract of land in District and County and State above, on Livingston Road and R. Stones line with line of Zacharies to Wolf River with river to Hales line to A. Flowers line to Jas. Mullins line. We covenant with Rolin Flowers and his heirs to defend title. Signed 23 Sept. 1851 Signed Levi (X) Flowers. Ursula (X) Flowers. William H. (X) Flowers. Witnessess - Rolin Story. Reaben Felkins. Examination taken of Usula Flowers apart from her husband relative to foregoing, 23 Sept. 1851. Signed, W. H. Turner, clerk. She was examined privately from her husband Levi Flowers. J. Bekman, J. P. The witnesses also proved the record in Overton County Court 8 March 1852. W. H. Turner, clerk.

Note: Sampson Williams who was prominent and lived in Jackson County, Tennessee, was a party to many and varied transactions in Overton County for a number of years prior to his death. ERW.

Minutes, Circuit Court 1815-24, Page 148. Sept. 14, 1818. The due Execution of a Deed of conveyance from Moses Williams to John Huff for four acres of land was this day proven in open court by the oaths of Daniel Hoff and Phillip Huff subscribing witnesses thereto and ordered to be recorded. The due execution of a Deed of conveyance from Moses Williams to John Huff for four acres of land was this day proven in open court by the oaths of Daniel Hoff and Phillip Hoff, subscribing witnesses thereto which was ordered to be certified. The due Execution of a deed of conveyance from Moses Williams to John Huff for sixteen acres of land was this day proven in open court by the oaths of Daniel Hoff and Philip Hoff subscribing witnesses thereto which was ordered to be certified.

Minutes, Circuit Court 1815-1824, Page 288. 1820. Strother Fogg VS John Huff and wife. Suit dismissed.

Minutes, Circuit Court 1815-1824, Page 44. Saturday 16 March. Martin Sim VS Phillip Huff .... In Chancery, This day came the plaintiff by his Council, and it appearing to the satisfaction of the court that the Defendant is an Inhabitant of the State of Kentucky, It is ordered that the publication be made in the Mountain Echo and Reporter, printed in Kentucky, for six weeks in session between now and the next term of this court, requiring the defendant to appear and answer, otherwise this cause will be set for hearing exparte at the next term of this court & c.

Minutes, Circuit Court 1815-1824, Page 71. 1817. Martin Sims VS Phillip Huff, Injunction Bill.

Minutes, Circuit Court 1815-1824, Page 91. March 15, 1817

Phillip Huff VS Daniel Adams. Demurer to scirifacias.

Minutes, Circuit Court, 1815-1824, Page 157. Sept. 1818. Phillip Huff VS Daniel Adams. Debt.

Minutes, Circuit Court 1815-1824, Page 177. 1818. Martin Sims complainant VS Phillip Huff, Injunction. Bill charged about 1812 complainant purchased of the Defendant a Salt Petre Cave in the County of Overton for which he executed a note.

Minutes, Circuit Court 1815-1824, Page 230. 1819 Sept. 15. The State VS Philip Hoff. Indictment for Perjury.

Marriages in Overton County, 1838-60 (Misc. Book) Page 54 Sept. 27 (28) 1841 Nathan Williams to Eliza A. Martin. By C. S. Wood. E.M.E.C.

Marriages 1838-60 (Misc. Book) Page 256. No.85. Dec. 29, 1852 Nathan Williams to Mary A. Butler, by T. Hale J.P. Jany 1, 1853.

Deeds G, Page 199. John M. Turner and wife Patience Turner, formerly Patience McDonald, petitions the court regarding dower of Elizabeth McDonald, Senr., widow of Michael Mc-Donnold, decd, out of lands in Overton County on Iron Creek. ---- 1832 ---- The widow received the mansion house and Mill and some land. In the division Lot No.1. went to Polly Hill; Lot No.2. to Sally McDonnold. Lot No.3. to Nancy Heard (Hoard), Lot No.4. to Elizabeth McDonnold. Lot No.5, to Thomas H. McDonnold. Lot No.6. to John McDonnold. Lot No.7, to Patience and John M. Turner. Lot No.8, to Fereby McDonnold. and Lot No.9 to James P. McDonnold. reported 26 January 1836.

Deeds C, Page 5. 15 March 1810. Charles Simmons of Washington County, Mississippi Territory, to John Harris of Overton County, Tennessee, 75 acres SE side Kettle Creek, Overton County.

Deeds C, Page 16. Henry Neeland (signed Neal at the end of record), Lydia Neel his wife, Joseph Terrell, Nancy Ferguson and Susanna McQueston all of Orange County, North Carolina, for good cause and consideration moving, nominate and appoint Janeral (General ?) Nathaniel Taylor of Carter County, Tennessee, our attorney to transact business for us as heirs at law of William Terrell, decd Nov. 25, 1811. Signed by all. Acknowledged in Orange County, N. C.

Deeds C, Page 21. Ambrose Lipscomb of Overton County, Tennessee, Power of attorney to Wiley Huddleston of Buckingham County, Virginia, executor of my brother Josiah Lipscomb decd, to receive my portion of estate coming to me. Oct.31, 1812.

Deeds C, Page 65. Nov. 10, 1812, Samuel Smith and Samuel Terry of Bladsoe County, Tennessee, to Daniel Sain of Overton County, 105 acres on waters of West Fork of Obed's River.

Deeds C, Page 94. 27 May 1812. Joseph Crawford of Overton County, deeds 300 acres to Evin Todhunter, March 1813.

Deeds C, Page 117. 17 April 1813. David Mebane and John Thompson, Executors of the last Will of James Mebane, late of Orange County, North Carolina, deceased, of one part and Henry Reagan of Overton County, Tennessee. Regards land in Overton Co., Tenn.

Deeds C, Page 219. George Teeter and Ester Teeter, his wife, late Ester Totten and former widow of Benjamin Totten, decd, George Hohemer and Easter Hohimer, late Ester Totten, James Totten, Joseph H. Totten, Parris Teeter and Richard Teeter, his wife, late Rebeccah Totten, children and legatees of Benjamin Totten, decd, appoint Benj. Totten our attorney, etc. Rebecca was the wife of Parris Teeter and Easter was the wife of George Teeter. 19 July 1813. Proved in Garrard County, Kentucky.

Deeds B, Page 14, Indenture 12 April 1809. Charles Hudspeth of Overton County, 443 acres on Lower side of Obed's River, sells to Leonard Davis of Surry County, North Carolina.

Deeds B, Page 41. March 12, 1808. Robert Hunt of the town of Newbern, in North Carolina, sells 1257 acres of land on West fork of Obed's River to John Harmore (Harmon ?) of Tennessee.

Deeds B, Page 43. Asahel Rawlings, Junior, of Roane County, Tennessee, appoint Daniel Alexander, Esquire, of White County, Tennessee, my attorney in fact for me and my name to let to John Eldridge of Overton County, certain land. Dec. 24, 1808.

Deeds B, Page 76. Indenture 3 July 1809 Samuel A. Martin of Lincoln County, North Carolina, to James Henderson of Rutherford County, Tennessee, 100 acres NW side Obed's River.

Deeds B, Page 77. Indenture 18 Nov. 1808 Samuel A. Martin of Rockingham County N.C. to Wm. Dale of Overton County, Tenn. 449 acres.

Deeds B, Page 83. Indenture 16 July 1795, Stockley Donelson of Knox County, Tennessee, William Terrell of said County and territory of one part, and John Lowe of Prince William County, Virginia, Josiah Watson of Alexandria and Samuel Lowe of Loudon County, Virginia, 40000 acres land in "Donelson's Cove" Overton County, Tennessee.

Deeds B, Page 101. Edward Carmack of Jackson County, Tennessee, 16 July 1805 to Thomas Dardis 800 acres on Wolf River, Overton County, Tennessee.

Deeds B, Page 120. Hugh Patrick of Overton County, for and in consideration of "Natural Love and affection which I bear unto my son John Patrick" and for the consideration of $1.00 same acknowledged convey land in Overton County.

Deeds B, Page 131. Indenture 10 January 1810. Joel Rice of Davidson County, Tennessee, to Solomon Debow of Caswell County, North Carolina, 4,266 acres of land on waters of Roaring River, Three tracts of land, 66 acres in Overton County, formerly Jackson County, being land granted by North Carolina to John Rice and levied on.

Deeds B, Page 133. Indenture January 8, 1810, Nathan Wood of White County, Tennessee, sells 100 acres North side of Spring Creek to Jesse Lovelady of Overton County, Refers to Lovelady's Spring Branch.

Deeds B, Page 138. Solomon Halling of Town of Newbern, in Craven County, North Carolina, for consideration of 300 pounds current money, Deeds 1257 acres of land on waters of Cumberland River to Robert Hunt of same place. 30 May 1795.

Deeds B, Page 140. Indenture 17 November 1809. Felps Reed of Grainger County, Tennessee, Deeds 600 acres on the Head of Lick Creek, to John McDonnold, of Overton County.

Deeds B, Page 148. Indenture 9 December 1809. Francis Mayberry of Grainger County, Tennessee, deeds 333 acres on both sides of Wolf River to John Ferby (Ferly ?) of Knox County, Tennessee.

Deeds B, Page 151. Indenture 2 December 1805. George Gordon of Green County, 400 acres on Eagle Creek to Jacob Meek of Jackson County, Tennessee.

Deeds B, Page 213. Jesse Hinshaw, Benjamin Hinshaw, and Jacob Hunshaw for causes and consideration moving appoint George Hinshaw our brother our attorney to convey lands in our names, 20 August 1811.

Deeds B, Page 221. Indenture 29 January 1811. Joseph Crawford of Overton County, Tennessee to Anthony Flowers of same 74 acres in said county.

Deeds B, Page 230. 12 Sept. 1810. John Hinds, Senr, of Knox County, Tennessee to Levi Hinds of Overton County, 260 acres of land on Wolf River.

Deeds B, Page 236. Thomas Houghton of Greene County, Georgia gives power of attorney to Jesse Standifer to transact business in Tennessee 8 March 1811.

Deeds B, Page 238. Jesse Standifer of Greene County, Georgia, Power of attorney to Henry Reagan of Overton County Tennessee, to sell land granted to Thomas Houghton by North Carolina land in Overton County, Tennessee. 4 May 1811.

Deeds B, Page 244. Indenture Sept. 2, 1811. Daniel Liles of Overton County, Tennessee to Jonathan Davis of Knox County, Tenn, 55 acres on Mitchell's Creek in Overton County.

Deeds B, Page 245. James Hogin Junr, deeds 150 acres on Obed's River to Young Hogin, March 1811.

Deeds B, Page 252. Our brother John Rice late of Nashville, Davidson County, Tennessee, decd, died intestate, Previous to his death said John, contracted with sundry persons for certain lands in Western Country and obligated himself to made deeds of conveyance. This is to make good his contract, Nathan Rice and William H. Rice both of Caswell County, North Carolina nominate and appoint Joel Rice and Elisha Rice our true and lawful attornies to convey said lands which we are entitled from said John Rice decd. We relinquish our right of administration to John and Elisha Rice. Signed Nathan Rice, William H. Rice. April 16, 1792.

Deeds B, Page 255. Copy of John Rice's will, on file here. (In part) I am indebted to Francis Ballard a horse and 16 lbs Virginia money. My horses are in Caswell County, North Carolina. Two are in the hands of Thomas Rice; one in the hands of Charles Taylor; one in the hands of Tilman Dixon. Debt due Absalom Tatum be paid. There is a debt due me from the State upward of 300 lbs, for Soldier's Service in the Continental Army. A debt due me from John Taylor. A debt due me from Estate of John Cuthral decd. My land called Chickasaw Bluff to belong to Elisha Rice because he is willing to go to Western Country. Each of my brothers to have their choice of land. My sisters to have 5000 acres of land divided amongst them. Jesse Benton to have next choice of 6000 acres of land. Certain land to be appropriated to use of schooling the poor at Cumberland. Appoints Co. Anthony Bledsoe, Jesse Benton, William H. Rice and Elisha Rice, executors. 14 June 1784. Signed John Rice. Proved in Davidson County, Tennessee, 1806.

Deeds B, Page 278. Isaac Burris of Overton County, Tennessee appoints and ordains Thomas Burris, my attorney, and behalf to demand and receive of John Meekey and Hawkey Forguson, the executors or Administrators of the estate Will and Testament of William Forguson, deceased.

Deeds B, Page 290. March 20, 1811. John C. Bedford of County of Cumberland, Kentucky, to William Nevens, 168 acres land on Bettle Creek.

Deeds B, Page 297. July 9, 1813. Josiah Patty of Blount County, Tennessee, to Joseph French of County of Knox, 153 acres of land on Wolf River.

Deeds B, Page 305. 4 March 1815. Leonard Harmon and Jordan Nipper of Grainger County, Tennessee, 105½ acres of land on Wolf River.

Deeds B, Page 306. Feby 1, 1808 George Gordon of Green County, Tenn. to John Sconce of Cumberland County, Kentucky, 300 acres North side Obed's River in Overton County, Tenn.

Deeds B, Page 323. 27 August 1813 Samuel McGee of Giles County, Tenn. to Andrew Hisaw of Overton County, Tenn. 150 acres on Yockums Creek.

Deeds B, Page 336. Arthur Fogg of Cumberland County in a deed.

Deeds B, Page 337. Wake County, North Carolina. Henry W. Rhodes of said county Bill of Sale four Negroes to Thomas Cope. Oct. 27, 1814.

Deeds B, Page 340. Thomas Cope senr of Overton County in consideration of "love and affection for my beloved daughter Elizabeth wife of William Hill", I convey and transfer two negroes. Aug. 22, 1815.

Deeds B, Page 341. Thomas Cope of Overton County for "love and affection toward my beloved daughter Sybia Hill wife of Thomas Hill" deeds negro girl. 22 August 1815.

Deeds B, Page 343. Indenture Oct. 3, 1815. Henry Lee, Patsy Conner, John Lee, Sarah Stewart and Mary Lee of Overton County, Tennessee, heirs and representatives of John Lee late of Washington County, State of Virginia decd, of one part to the heirs of Tobias McNew decd of the other part. 50 acres of land on north fork of Holston. All sign. (Recorded in Overton County, but does not seem to regard land in Overton County.)

Deeds A, Page 5. Indenture Nov. 11, 1806. Joseph Hart of the county of Blount in Tennessee to William Douglass of Knox County, Tenn. 300 acres for $300. Undivided part of a certain tract of land granted to William Douglass, John Sharp, John McAllister, Thomas Hart, 100 acres, Middle District on waters of Roaring River.

Deeds A, Page 16. John Sevier of Knox County, Tennessee, 56 acres of land to John Coons of Jackson County, Tennessee. 15 March 1806 land in Jackson County and Overton County.

Deeds A, Page 22. November 5, 1804. Samuel Scott of Orange County, North Carolina, deeds 5000 acres to Simon Huddleston of Jackson County, for $1500, Land between Wolf and Obed's Rivers.

Deeds A, Page 23. 26 June 1806. Abraham Goodpasture Senr, of Jackson County, Tennessee, 100 acres to John Goodpasture of same, land on waters of Roaring River.

Deeds A, Page 32. William Terrell of Fredericksburg, Virginia, late of Knox County, Tennessee, appoints James Easton of Raleigh, North Carolina, attorney to sell land on Obed's River. 12 January 1798.

Deeds A, Page 33. William Terrell of Knox County, on 14 March, 1800, as attorney in fact for James Easton of Raleigh, North Carolina, and Thomas Dillon of the town of Lynchburg, Virginia, refers to survey of 5000 acres including Fendlestones Spring. Refers to Robert Young, Hawkins County, Tenn. North side Clinch River about five miles NW of Richard Henderson and Cos. in Powell's Valley, etc.

Deeds A, Page 40. Thomas Dillon deed to William Dillen 833 acres October, 1806. Thomas Dillen of Davidson County, and William Dillen of Overton County.

Deeds A, Page 51. 6 August 1806. Oliver Smith of Pitt County, North Carolina, and Nancy his wife of one part and Moses Fisk of the County of Jackson, Tennessee for and in consideration of the sum of $480.00 conveys 640 acres land in Jackson County, on eastern branch of Roaring River. 640 acres granted by North Carolina to Nancy Shephard now the wife of said Oliver Smith by patent No. 2293. dated 20 May 1793.

Deeds A, Page 85. John Sevier of Knox County and George Gordon of Greene County, Tenn., to Jesse Bond of Jackson County, Tenn., 200 acres land 20 March 1806.

Deeds V, Pages 158-59. April 20, 1866. L. C. Copeland, G. A. Copeland, B. A. Copeland, L. F. M. Copeland, A. C. Copeland, and J. D. Walker, Mary Ann Walker his wife of Overton County, Tennessee. T. J. Copeland & Co. aforesaid. The first group for and in consideration of $100 each paid by L. J. Copeland same hereby acknowledged, convey right title undivided interest in a to certain tract of land in said county on waters of Mathews Creek, a branch of Roaring River Containing 350 acres. It was a tract granted to Sampson Williams. Also another survey in name of Philip Copeland. Signed Larkin C. Copeland, G. A. J. Copeland, B. A. Copeland, F. M. Copeland, A. C. Copeland, James D. Walker, M. A. Walker (X); Nelly Ellender (X)Copeland; Emeline F. Copeland. All proved in Overton County.

Deeds M, Page 104. 21 April 1852. William C. Hall survivor

of the firm of Ferguson & Hall of Albany, and in the State of North Carolina, etc. etc. referred to.

Deeds G, Page 213. 14 January 1836. Henry Graham and John Graham Junr of one part heirs at law of John Graham decd and James Mullins of other part, all of Overton County, consideration of $60.00 to John Graham deceased in hands. Signed Henry (X) Graham. John Graham. 26 Jany 1836.

Deeds G, Page 230. March 11, 1836. Thomas Davis of Overton County, to Hugh Roberts, John Stone, Matthew Davis, Isaac Davis and William Davis of Jackson and Overton Counties, for $1125, paid. To Thomas Davis. Sell land of Leonard Davis their father 443 acres. Land on Sycamore Stump on bank of Obed River lower end L. Davises Plantation. Signed by all.

Deeds N, Page 445. John Wright and Mary Wright his wife and Thomas McDonald and Susanna McDonald his wife and Jonnathan Hunt and Milly his wife, and Elizabeth Jane Hunt, for and in consideration of $166.65 paid, each by Jessee Roberts, convey deliver to said Roberts all the right title claim Interest we have as heirs and distributees of John Hunt decd, in a negro boy named Henry, belonging to estate of John Hunt decd, January 24, 1857. All sign.

Deeds N, Page 493. 19 June 1826. James Chisum of Hardiman County, Tennessee, to George Maxwell of Overton County, deeds 100 acres land on waters of Spring Creek in Overton County, adjoining dower lands of widow Ramsey's old place. Signed James Chism.

Deeds N, Page 11. Indenture ...... consideration $35.00 paid --- William C. West, Tench McCormack, Catherine his wife, Joseph Brown and Sally his wife, Reuben West and Anderson West and Polly his wife, Henry W. West, all of Overton County, sell to William C. West their undivided interest in estate of Isaac West, Esq., decd, of Overton County. Refers to several different undivided interests and some in land on Matthew Creek in Overton County, including dwelling house. 1 May 1848. All sign.

Deeds N, Page 55. George W. Stone, John Stone, and Rebecca Stone sell convey to Nancy Stone and her heirs for $300. all their interest in land of John Stone, deceased, being three sevenths of one Sixth part of same, Subject to dower interest of said Nancy widow of said John Stone decd. Land in Overton County. District No.4. containing in all 453 acres in different tracts. 15 June 1855. All sign.

Deeds I, Page 317. Indenture 12 Nov. 1838. Between William Chilton and Benjamin Flowers both of Overton County for and in consideration of $100 paid to William Flemming. Chilton conveys to Flowers tract of land on waters of Obed's River, on Eagle Creek containing 120 acres. Adjoins Thomas Hill.

Deeds N, Page 348. We, James A. Stone, Sarah Stone, William Garhart, Sarah Garhart, N. H. Caldwell, Nancy Caldwell, Jonathan Roberts and Bennett Stone guardian of James B. and Joseph B. Roberts of Tennessee quit claim all right title and interest in and to a tract of land on Sharted branch adjoining land of Sarah Bowman in District No.3, of Overton County, described in deed from Jackson Burchett and Eliza Burchet to M. M. Williams made 4 Feby 1856, except the land deeded from Hugh Roberts to Sarah I. Roberts, and Matilda I. Forbes. Signed 25 Sept. 1856. Signed N. H. Caldwell, I. A. Stone, Wm. Garhart, Nancy Caldwell, Sarah Garhart and Sarah Stone. All acknowledged in Overton County.

Deeds N, Page 60. Will of Martin Garrett. deceased. The said will not being signed the heirs confirmed the will by articles signed by all of them. Legatees who signed, Esther (X) Garrett. Arthur G. Garrett. Jacob L. Garrett. Elizabeth (X) Garrett. Will says -- "I Martin Garrett of Overton County, Tennessee" want to be buried at my father in the family graveyard in this county. Wife Esthar L. Garrett $50.00 and household goods. Place I now live on. Sons Arthur G. Garrett and Jacob L. Garrett land. To Elizabeth J. Garrett land bought of Hinton J. Staggs. Appoints R. N. Goodpasture executor. May 24 1855. Proved July 2 1855.

Deeds N, Page 87. Thomas Eldridge, James Eldridge, Z. Eldridge, Jefferson Eldridge, Catherine (X) McCormack, George McCormack, deed undivided 20 acres lying on waters of Roaring River to Calvin Eldridge for consideration of "love and affection." Quit claim. 7 May 1855.

Deeds N, Page 101. Indenture April 30, 1851. Joseph Edward and Lettia Edwards of Davis County, Iowa, and Henry P. Buford of Skyler County, Missouri, their attorney, sells 150 acres in District No.4 to B. W. Stephens, for $120. All sign.

Deeds N, Page 117. Thomas Hardy on 25 August 1843. Conveyed to His daughters Nancy Langford, Sally Gore, and Elizabeth Gore, certain tract of land, tenents in common. We, Phillip Gore and his wife Sally, Claiborne Gore and his wife Elizabeth, convey an equally divident to Ruffus W. Langford, Senr, and wife Nancy, Phillip and Claiborne and wives convey to Ruffus this land. 15 December 1851. All sign.

Deeds N, Page 154. Indenture 14 February 1854. Henry James and Elizabeth late Miller, wife formerly of Abraham Miller, and Henry James of Allen County, Kentucky, to Bennett Hargrave of Overton County, Tennessee, 100 acres near Little Eagle Creek, District No.7, Overton County. Proved in Allen County, Kentucky, 14 Feby 1854.

Deeds N, Page 65. M. M. Williams in penal sum of $400 condition of Obligation, we sold M. M. Williams a tract of land on waters of Shasteens (?) Branch in Overton County, Tenn. 28 March 1855. Signed A. J. Burchart, Eliza (X) Burchart.

Deeds S, Page 448. Ailsey Burley deed of conveyance in third District of Overton County, Tennessee to Thomas E. Hays, for and in consideration of $450. a tract of land in Overton County, Land adjoining James Williams, on side of Fish Road. Adjoining Simeon Hinds tract. And on Lick Creek. 1867 Sept. 14, Signed Ailsey Burley. Witnesses, Elijah Johnson, Joseph Martin. Proved Sept.30, 1867.

Deeds N, Page 374. Archibald B. Hays, and Neomy Hays, formerly Wilson, his wife, being lawful heirs of Joseph Wilson decd, sold A. G. Speck for and in consideration of the sum of $10.00 paid, 14 and six-fourteenths acres on the West fork of Obed's River. Interest claim and etc. that we have in and to the dower of the widow of said Wilson, decd. 10 October 1856. Signed A. B. Hays. Neomy (X) Hays. Witnesses, Jas. A. Richardson, G. W. Speck.

Deeds N, Page 514. Bennett Hargrave 6 Sept. 1851 of Overton County to Nancy McMillen of said county, Dist. 7. 100 acres on waters Eagle Creek.

Deeds N, Page 515. John Gerlin and Arty Gerlin, formerly Arty Hays have this day bargain and sold to S. L. Hays and heirs for consideration $50.00 paid. all interest in a tract of land to which we may be Entitled therein the said Arty Gerlin as heir of W. C. Hays and the said John Gerlin husband of the said Arty in Overton County, Tennessee, in District No.3, containing 219 acres of land adjoining Joseph Pharris and Elijah Johnson and by Joseph Martin and Thomas Maxwell and on west adjoins Maxwell, Squire Dillen and Thomas Dillen and W. S. Harris. 6 April 1857. Signed John Gerlin, Arty (X) Gerlin. Attest. Wm. Pharris, Thomas E. Hays. Same proved.

Deeds R, Page 316. October 12th, 1865. We hereby convey for ourselves and our heirs unto Jonathan D. Hale and his heirs the tract of land on which Mary Poor now lives and lying in the County of Overton and State of Tennessee on Obeys River and bounded as follows being on T. Garrotts line on the River Running with his line to Mrs. McClennings line and with her line to Jas. Ommenetts line and with his line to Taylors line and with Taylors line to Garretts line and with Garretts line to the beginning point. 300 acres more or less. Hale within one year to pay $600.00. Signed Mary Poor, Nercisis Hill.
Witnesses. Thomas K. Parkinson. Orville D. Hardy. Proved in Smith County, Tennessee, October 26, 1865.
NOTE: I think the name Ommenetts in the above intended for Emmetts but it is clearly as given herein. ERW.

Deeds R, Page 405. Indenture 31st March 1865. W. M. Poore

to McMillin. Lease of 150 acres land on waters of Lick Creek in Overton County on Obed's River. Civil District No.8 all timber. Signed W. M. Poor, J. H. McMillen. Witnesses - J. P. Johnson. Sarah & M. C. Poor. Benton McMillen. James Whitesides. Same Proved in County court.

Deeds Q, Page 82. Mary Poor lease to F. E. Beck. Leases 400 acres for consideration of $1.00 which is acknowledged and $200 when well of oil is obtained producing 50 pounds or more. Land on Obey's River the farm on which Mrs. Poor now lives 450 acres more or less adjoining H. Talors land and Mccllens (?) land and H. Clarks land and Shadrack Garretts land. Dig for coal oil or other minerals. Lease for 30 years. May 3, 1865. Signed Mary Poor. F. E. Beck. Attest - Levi (X) Clark. Shadrack Garrett. Proved in Overton County.

Deeds A, Page 59 (old book 73) Robr. Hays D. S. to Report of Survey Nancy Sheppard .... District of Mero, Sumner County, By virtue of a military warrant from the Secretary of the State of North Carolina No.2084 date of Entry 29, Oct. 1792. I have surveyed for Nancy Sheppard Assee one mally of the heirs of Daniel Rogers, 640 acres of land supposed to be and be situated on the Eastern branches of Roaring River near the head, beginning at a beech and buckeye on the west side of a branch, running thence west three hundred and twenty polls to an ash, thence north three hundred and twenty poles to a stake, thence east 320 poles to a stake, thence south 320 poles to the beginning. Signed 20th Novr. 1792. Robert Hays D. S. Marte Armstrong Sur.

Deeds A, Page 333 (Orig A, Page 414). State of North Carolina Grant No.2041 for 640 acres on Thompson's Creek. Patsy Thompson Hays. State of North Carolina No.2041. Know ye, that we have granted unto Patsy Thompson Hays, assignee of Francis Berry, a private in the Continental Line of aforesaid State, 640 acres land in our County of Sumner on Thompson Creek, the waters of Roaring River, beginning at a cherry tree and dogwood, runs North three hundred and twenty poles to an oak, then East 320 poles to a stake, then South 320 poles to a stake; then west 320 poles to the beginning, To hold to the said Patsy Thompson Hays, her heirs and assigns forever. Dated the 20th day of May 1793. Signed Richd Dobbs Spaight. J. Glasgow. Sec. Copy from the records. Test - Will White, Sec. Registered 29th Dec. 1808.

Deeds B, Page 129. N. C. Grant No.2041 to Patsy Thompson Hays assee of Francis Berry, tract of land 640 acres Sumner County.

Deeds B, Page 285. Tennessee Grant No.2286. for 10 acres on Caney Fork of Wolf River, to James Davisson, Land District No.4. No.874 dated 17 April 1811. Warrant No.1358 to John Carter and John Foster, 300 acres, 4 May 1792 and vested in Nathaniel Taylor by purchase at Sheriff Sale.

Deeds B, Page 287. Tennessee Grant No.2154. 89 acres on waters of Lick Creek to James Davisson. District No.4. No.875 founded on warrant No.1358 issued by John Carter and John Foster, for 300 acres 1 May 1792. Entry dated 17 May 1811. for 100 acres issued to James Davisson the Enterer. 89 acres in District of Winchester, on waters of Lick Creek near Colonel Chisman's line.

Deeds M, Page 284. Blair R. Davidson from Doak H. Capps.

Deeds D, Page 309. James Davidson, Tennessee Grant.

Deeds D, Page 22. William Gibson of Overton County to Stephen Senter of Roane County, Tennessee. Indenture 24 June 1813, for 50 acres on Caney Fork and said Cumberland Road, the consideration being $780. including place said Gibson now lives.

Deeds D, Page 29. Thomas Cope of Overton County, conveys one negro 7 years old named Mariah to Molly Cope for love and affection for my daughter, 22 August 1815. Signed Thomas Q. Cope. Adam Huntsman. Joseph Harris.

Deeds D, Page 43. William Earp to Timothy Carpenter, 300 acres in Poplar Creek on waters of Obed's River. 1816.

Deeds B, Page 49. Jacob Anderson sells 160 acres to Moses Fisk Anderson of Jackson County. 1806.

Deeds B, Page 54. Power of Attorney Joseph McEludth of Sumner County, Tennessee, and Martin Young, power of attorney to Henry Reagan, Esq., of Overton County, To sell land 1816.

Deeds D, Page 66. 21 February 1814. Robert D. Pierce of Campbell County, Tennessee to Nathan Cooper of Overton County, 7 acres of land in Overton County.

Deeds D, Page 100. Indenture 24 August 1816, Samuel Fulton of Washington County, Virginia to Benjamin Estill of County and State aforesaid, deeds two tracts of land. Refers to heirs of Lewis Shell; to Marca Gill; to James Orr; to William Graham; to James McCue; to Alexr. Smith; to John Granden; to Thomas Tate; to Peter Scott; James Herley, William Tate; William Snodgrass; James Meek guardian of children of Stephen Meek; James Campbell, Sr.; John Lowry; Sadler David Bucknan; James Fulton; Silbourn Henderson; Andrew Russell Senr. Refers to will of Alex Givens of Augusta County, Virginia. This is a very, very long record.

Deeds D, Page 107. Indenture 11 May 1816, Thomas Jackson of Hawkins County, Tennessee sells 350 acres of land on west fork of Obed's River to Menan M. Martin of Overton County, Tennessee.

Deeds D, Page 115. Thomas Dillen of Davidson County, Tennessee, to Moses Fisk of Overton County, 177 acres Flatt Creek in Overton County. 1820.

Deeds D, Page 120. George W. Sevier of Overton County, power of attorney to Walter King of Roane County, Refers to land of Moses Caveat. 1817.

Deeds D, Page 130. Christian Baker of Overton County, conveys 153 acres to Josiah Patty of Blount County, Tennessee. 1808.

Deeds D, Page 131. Henry Regan (Reagan) Admr. of Estate of John Beatty, decd, bill of sale 4 negroes - Lucy, Jacob, Nancy and Anis - to Thomas H. Harris, 17 August 1816. Witnessed by Joseph Poor, Samuel Odle, John Thurman.

Deeds D, Page 131. Wm. Bradshaw and wife Elizabeth of Overton County, for 420 pounds sells Wm. Buch (Beech) slaves. 1813.

Deeds D, Page 135. Indenture March 10, 1815, Samuel McGee of Giles County, Tennessee, to George Coalter of Lincoln County, Tennessee, sells 150 acres land Yochane's Creek (Yoakum Creek), a branch of Wolf River, Overton County, Tenn

Deeds D, Page 136. November 22, 1816. Thomas Jackson of Hawkins County, Tennessee, deeds 157 acres Eagles Creek, to John Coones, Senr., of Overton County.

Deeds D, Page 149. Indenture 24 October 1816. Anthony Dibrell of White County, Tenn., to Alex. Officer of Overton County, 100 acres of land in Overton County on Obed's River.

Deeds D, Page 151. Indenture 11 October 1817. James Mayfield of Overton County, to Will Whitsides of Madison County, Territory of Illinois, one half of undivided moiety in 800 acres in Madison County, Illinois, for consideration of $200. it being obtained by virtue of my donation right granted to me by being head of a family in Illinois in the year 1788, etc.

Deeds D, Page 154. Walter Greer, Ann Greer and Stephen Copeland, a negro girl to James McDonald.

Deeds D, Page 155. 18 October 1817. David Mebane, James Mebane and John Thompson, Executor, of last Will and Testament of James Mebane, late of Orange County, N. C., decd. David Mebane of Orange County, N. C. to George Allen Mebane. Refers to agreement of Henry Rowan of Hawkins County, Tenn.

Deeds D, Page 169. Indenture 8 November 1816. Felps Reed of Grainger County, Tennessee, and the widow and heirs of John Beaty, decd, of Overton County. 300 acres land in

Overton County.

Deeds D, Page 204. Indenture May 14, 1818. William Alexander of Mecklenburg County, North Carolina, power of attorney to John Bowen; His attorney sells Edward Durant land in Overton County, May 14 1818. Refers to Grant to Andrew Alexander, decd.

Deeds D, Page 210. Josiah Collins the Elder of the town of Edenton, North Carolina, deeds 1280 acres on Bear Creek to David Barrons of Edgecombe County, North Carolina. The land in Overton County, Tennessee.

Deeds D, Page 214. Indenture 4 December 1797. John Gaddy of Franklin County, North Carolina, deeds 6280 acres of land on Obed's River and Bear Creek to Josiah Collins of the Town of Edenton, North Carolina. Proved in North Carolina.

Deeds D, Page 225. David Beaty of Overton County, Tennessee, appoints Alexander Beaty of Cumberland County, Kentucky, his attorney, 1817.

Deeds D, Page 228. United States of America, James Monroe, President, grant on Warrant No.12614, 160 acres to Isaac Baugh, late a private in Hawkins Co., In 17th Regiment of Infantry, Baugh was in the late army of the United States. The land in the Territory of Illinois. Recorded in the General Land Office of the U. S. (NOTE: There is no explanation as to why it was recorded in Overton County, Tennessee.)

Deeds D, Page 238. Indenture April 14, 1818. John Southgate of the Borough of Norfolk, in Virginia, sells 3552 acres of land to Moses Fisk.

Deeds D, Page 246. Indenture 28 October 1816. Polly Anderson, Admrx. of the Estate of Robert Anderson decd., of Overton County, to David Whetchel, 75 acres of land on head waters of Roaring River.

Deeds D, Page 265. Indenture 26 Oct. 1818. Valentine Matlock, Sheriff of Overton County, to David Burford of Smith County, Tennessee, and Henry H. Atkinson of Overton County, 10240 acres of land.

Deeds D, Page 278. North Carolina. William Davis of Surry County, North Carolina, consideration moving appoints William Masters of Overton County, Tennessee, power of attorney. to sell land in Overton County, on Roaring River. 1817.

Deeds D, Page 320. Indenture 27 January 1818. Thomas Simpson executor of the last will and Testament of Samuel Tate, deceased, of one part and John Tate Senr, both of Overton

County, Simpson the executor of the last will and Testament of Samuel Tate sells a tract of land 40 acres on Roaring River.

Deeds D, Page 334, Samuel Smith of Bledsoe County power of attorney to sell land in Overton County, Tenn, including the place Ezekiel Pauther formerly lived known by name Big Cane Brake. Power of attorney to Adam Huntsman, 1813.

Deeds D, Page 349. October 28, 1816, John Williams, agent for heirs of John Williams, decd, of Overton County, sell to George Christian land on Roaring River.

Deeds D, Page 360. Edward Durant transfers personal property to Samuel Durant, April 30, 1819.

Deeds D, Page 371. Thomas Minor of Overton County, do give and bequeath confirm unto son Hiram Minor one half land whereon Thomas now resides. On Obed River. July 10, 1819.

Deeds D, Page 402. Moses Williams of Cumberland County, Kentucky, sells four acres land in Overton County, Tennessee, to Phillip Huff in 1819.

Deeds D, Page 403. Phillip Huff of Cumberland County, Kentucky, to Martin Sims of Wayne County, Kentucky, 3 acres land in Overton County, Tennessee.

Deeds D, Page 418. Margaret Officer of White County, Tennessee, bond for Title to Joseph Murphey of Overton County, 1814.

Deeds D, Page 423. 25 March 1793. Robert and Thomas King of Hawkins County, in District of "Territory South of the River Ohio", to David Ross of Fluvanna County, Virginia, 2500 acres land on Wolf River.

Deeds D, Page 309. State of Tennessee. Grant No.5046 for 22½ acres on Caney Fork of Wolf River to James Davidson, Sept. 5, 1815, in 4th District No.2384. Certificate No.475, by Anthony Foster to R. I. Taylor. 1827. 29 January 1811. 22½ acres of which an assignment to James Davidson.

Deeds D, Page 165. Indenture 20 August 1810. William Reneau of Overton County, to Moses Poor of same for and in consideration $1.00 paid by said Poor acknowledged conveys to Moses Poor his heirs a tract of land in Overton County whereon said Reneau now lives, conveyed to said Reneau by William Chilton agent for George Gordon. Land adjoining McDonald's line, 65 acres. Signed William Reneau.

Deeds D, Page 382. Bill & decree. Divesting George Gordon and vesting Wm. Chilton, with the lands herein described. One half undivided moiety of 32000 acres land on Obed's River granted by the State of North Carolina to John Sevier and George Gordon.

Court in town of Monroe Second Monday in March 1819 before Hon. Circuit Court of Law and Equity, held for the County of Overton, December 1817 William Chilton filed his bill of complaint, in said court which is in the following words and figures --- William Chilton complaining, represents that on or about the 16th day of June 1810, he made and entered into a contract with a certain George Gordon for one half of an undivided moiety of 32000 acres of land, granted by the State of North Carolina to John Sevier, lying and being in the County of Overton, on the waters of Obed's River, a branch of Cumberland River adjoining said John Sevier other survey of 25060 acres. George Gordon held by deed of conveyance from said John Sevier 10 Feby 1797 and registered in Sumner County and Knox County. Deed delivered to George Gordon. Gordon promised that he would come out from Green County where he lived and resided and acknowledged the due execution thereof in the County of Overton where the lands lay. Said Gordon was to come out for that purpose the same fall after said purchase but failed to do so. By some casualty or misfortune deed was lost and said George refuses to make another deed. claims George tried to cheat, etc. (very long record.)

Deeds D, Page 295. Power of attorney, Nancy Chowning, Mason Kelly and Sarah Kelly, Mildred Chowning, Barthena W. Chowning, Thomas Chandler, and Joannah Chandler, Gordon Brown, and Elsey S. Brown, being heirs at law of the late Thomas Chowning, Elder, decd, all of Overton County, Tennessee, appoint our brother William C. Chowning of said county our attorney, to sell land and attend to transaction of business. 200 acres of land seems to be involved which is in Henry County, Virginia, on east side of Smith's River. Jany 23, 1819. All sign.

Deeds D, Page 354. Indenture 28 April 1818. 100 acres, Peter Cherry, Benjamin Cherry, Harvey Cherry and James Russell all of Overton County, Tennessee, to Jacob Beason of same place. The consideration being $385.00 for tract of land in Overton County.

Deeds F, Page 1. Indenture 26 April 1827. William Chilton Senr., of Overton County, to Jacob Dillon of same. for consideration $100.00 conveys tract of land in Overton County on south side of Wolf River part in Fentress County. Both sides Wolf River now occupied by Henry Dillon. Signed Wm. Chilton.

Deeds F, Page 57. William Chilton Senr, letter of attorney William Jr, and John Chilton. William Chilton Senr, of Overton County, Tennessee, appoints my two sons William Chilton, Junr, and John Chilton or either of them my attorney to manage and conduct a matter of business regards a tract of land in Supreme Chancery court of the State of Virginia, at Lynchburg, in which I am complainant and Richard Chilton and others are Defendants. I authorize and appoint either of them in my name to transact all and any part of said suit or anything relating to same. Regards the: Obtain my distributive share of the Estate of my Father Richard Chilton as may be coming to me or such as I am entitled to, etc. Signed Wm. Chilton. 29 December 1829. Witnessed by George (X) Bock (Beck ?), John (X) Brown, Proved and recorded in Overton County, Tennessee.

Deeds F, Page 61. Indenture January 1830. John Chilton and Thomas Joust, executors of the last will and testament of George Armstrong (late of Overton County) of Overton County, deed to William Chilton, for consideration of $1200 paid by Wm. Chilton to said John and Thomas. Conveys to William Chilton certain negroes of Estate of George Armstrong, decd.

Deeds F, Page 98. William Chilton Jr. deeds two lots in town of Monroe to Thos. B. Hayter, for $700. Oct.10, 1828.

Deeds F, Page 119. William Chilton VS George Gordon in suit. Brought in court 1817.

Deeds F, Page 140. Wm. Chilton conveys 50 acres to Frederick Ammonett, land in Overton County, July 15, 1828.

Deeds F, Page 176. Chesley Taylor and other heirs and heirs at law of Edward Taylor bill of sale to William Chilton Jr. Indenture 1829 between Chesley Taylor, Spiecy Pryor, formerly Spicy Taylor and her husband William Pryor, and Massey Pryor, formerly Massey Taylor and her husband John Pryor, John Taylor, Hezekiah Taylor, David Taylor, Pleasant Taylor, Polly Taylor, Elizabeth Taylor heirs at law of Edward Taylor late of Virginia, and Elizabeth Taylor, the Elder, widow and relict of said Edward Taylor having a life estate in his property, of one part and William Children Junr of Overton County, Tennessee, for and in consideration of $500 paid, sell William Chilton a negro woman Eliza age about 16 years. Delivered to William Children 5 Feby 1829. All sign. Elizabeth Taylor, Jr. had a guardian. Teste - Elizah Garrott, Junr., Joel Parriss, Samuel G. Claborn, proved in Overton County, Tennessee.

Deeds F, Page 177. Indenture 5 Feby 1827. The consideration being $500, paid by William Chilton Jr, 150 acres on Obed River and this record again names all the Taylor heirs of Edward Taylor late of Virginia. Regards land in Overton County, Tenn.

Deeds F, Page 271. George C. Hays and Sarah D. Hays letters of Attorney sell lands in State of Missouri to Charles Hays.

Know all men, George C. Hays and Sarah D. Hays of Overton County, confiding in the prudence ability and integrity of Charles Hays of Adair County, Kentucky, make and appoint him Charles Hays our true and lawful attorney to sell convey and make title to all right claim interest and estate we have in lands which may come to us we have in the State of Missouri. March 24 1832. Signed G. C. Hays. Sarah D. Hays. Sarah was wife of G. C. Hays.

Deeds F, Page 279. John Sedwell of Marrion County, Tenn, to Joseph Tompkins of Overton County. 320 acres land Roaring River. 11 Nov. 1831.

Deeds F, Page 269. Martin Masters and William Masters, bill of Sale for negro slave Leethy to George C. Hays. Martin Masters and William Masters of Jackson County, Tennessee. for $300 paid sell G. C. Hays of Overton County a negro girl about 18 years of age. 1 June 1831.

Deeds F, Page 473. William L. Armstrong mortgage deed for negro girl Polly age about 5 years to George C. Hays. secure debt $208.24. March 20, 1834.

Deeds E, Page 241. (original book p.225) Indenture 22 Sept. 1817. Joseph Poor and John Long, both of Overton County, Tennessee, Joseph for and in consideration of the sum of $1000 paid by John Long conveys to said Long a tract of land 320 acres in said County on Three Forks of Wolf River Beginning on beginning corner of Walnut Grove tract except tract land reserved to Conrod Pile, etc. lane and school house by reversing said course. It seems that John Blair's land joins. Signed Joseph (X) Poor. Witnesses - Henry Reagan, Henry H. Atkinson, Joseph French, Wm. Chilton, Will Armstrong. Proved Jany court 1820.

Deeds E, Page 240 (224). Indenture 20 August 1817. Vincent Benhaw to Joseph Poor, both of Overton County for and in consideration of the sum of $1000 paid conveys to Joseph Poor 300 acres of land in said county, at three forks of Wolf River beginning on corner of Walnut Grove tract except certain tract reserved to Conrod Pile, etc. etc.

Deeds E, Page 363 (310). Indenture 27 October 1823. William Chilton of Overton County to Moses Poor of same in consideration of $14 paid William Chilton, conveys to Moses Poor tract of land in Overton County on waters of Wolf River part of tract of 32000 acres granted by North Carolina to John Sevier and conveyed to said William Chilton by George Gordon. Land adjoins Paynes, Signed Wm. Chilton. no witnesses.

Deeds E, Page 110. Sampson Williams to Joseph White Williams of Overton County, makes Joseph Williams power of attorney to convey and execute deed with Job and Reuben Carlock

21 Nov. 1817. for Land on Roaring River.

Deeds E, Page 40. State of North Carolina Grant No.2401. 1000 acres Know ye that we have granted unto Willoughby Williams assignee of the heirs of Oliver Williams a fifer in the Continental line of said State land in Middle District on East side of West fork of Obeys River. Beginning above a tract of Col. John Armstrong of 2750 acres. on bank of said River, etc. 5 Feby 1795. Signed Richard Dobbs Speight.

Deeds E, Page 23. Moses Fiske of Hilham in Overton County, deeds one acres of land to Andrew Donovan and Thomas Lea. One lot in town of Hilham, on south side of Public Road. Feby 22, 1819.

Deeds E, Page 31. John Barham of Madison County, Alabama, appoints friend Sampson Williams of Jackson County, Tennessee, attorney to sell land in Overton County, in town of Monroe. said land was conveyed by John McDonald to Thomas Overton and myself jointly by deed 6 Nov. 1818. John McDonald and McDonnold both spellings in this deed.

Deeds E, Page 58. William Armstrong, Senior, of Overton County for and in consideration of "love and good will and affection which I bear toward my loving daughter Peggy Senter wife of Stephen Senter" of said county, give, grant to Peggy Senter and legal heirs a negro girl now in her possession, etc. 15 Dec.1819. Signed Wm. Armstrong.

Deeds E, Page 59. William Armstrong gift to his daughter Nancy Gibbons wife of Epps Gibbons of said county. a negro slave. Jany 1820.

Deeds E, Page 65. Indenture 24 April 1820. Abraham Van Hooser of Overton County, Tennessee, deeds 80 acres to Andrew Carson heirs of. Land in Donelson Cove. Overton County.

Deeds E, Page 72. Indenture 9 April 1796. Henry Flewery, Merchant, in Bertie County, North Carolina, 800 acres to Reverend Charles Pettigrew of said county. Land in Sumner County, Tenn, on Roaring River.

Deeds E, Page 126. Indenture 25 August 1820. John McIver of Fairfax County, Virginia, 401¼ acres land to Jeremiah Odle decd, Margaret Odle. widow. John Odle, Samuel Odle, Sarah Odle, Rebecca Odle, Margaret Odle, children and heirs at law of Jeremiah Odle, decd. of Overton County, Tennessee.

Deeds E, Page 129. Will of David Ross of the City of Richmond, Virginia. To son Frederick Augustus Ross tract of land which I have put into the hands of my son David Ross, Junior, and slaves, etc. Son David, Junior, land named

Mount Ida and Red House plantation about 1400 acres, etc. My four children and their heirs, namely Eliza Myers wife of Jacob Myers, Amanda A. Duffield wife of John Duffield, Frederick A. Ross and David Ross, Junior. Appoints son F. A. Ross and Son in law Jacob Myers, executors and Thos. T. Bolden, executor. April 24, 1817. Signed David Ross. witnessed by John Jameson, Sewell Osgood, M. H. Rice, proved in Henrico County, Virginia 1818. (Note - This is a very long record.)

Deeds E, Page 159. Indenture April 1821 George Gordon of Green County, Tenn, by his attorney in fact William Chilton of Overton County sells Elizabeth Guthrie (Guthorie) land in Overton County, 50 acres.

Deeds E, Page 171. Indenture 1 Feby 1821. Elisha Walker, brother and Jeremiah Walker, and Francis Walker, heirs at law of James Walker, decd, to Thomas Faucher, 160 acres in Overton County. (Note - The name should be, I think,Fauncher instead of Faucher. ERW)

Deeds E, Page 173. George W. Sevier and Joseph H. Windle power of attorney to Samuel H. DeWolf esq., attorney at law Monroe County, Alabama, to handle certain business in Overton County, Tennessee 1821.

Deeds E, Page 173. Jonathan Ammerine of Maidson County, Kentucky, 202½ acres to Joseph Ashworth, 1821.

Deeds E, Page 175. Indenture Sept. 8, 1818 Joseph Cobb of Grainger County, Tennessee and wife Sarah to John Blair, 500 acres land for "natural love and affection we bear to said John Blair". Tract of land in Overton County, three forks of Wolf River. Land adjoining land granted in name of Catherine Blair 500 acres. Granted by North Carolina in name of John Blair.

Deeds E, Page 176. Will of Adam Craig of Richmond. wife Mary Craig. Household goods for her life. House and lot in Richmond. (I think it means Virginia.) now occupied by my family. My lands and plantation in Chickahomony. Son William M. Craig 71200 acres in Kentucky. (Military Grant.) Refers to William Mallory father of wife. Land in York County. All my children Wife Executrix. Friends William Marchal Sr., William Henry, Jr., John Foster, Mr. Samuel Payne. Dr. John Adams, Mr. Andrew Stephenson, Executors of this my last will and testament. Son James when of age. March 16, 1808. Proved in Richmond, Virginia 1808.

Deeds E, Page 180. March 3, 1814. Charles Simmons of Christian County, Kentucky, to Benjamin Boles. 213 acres land in Overton County, Tennessee.

Deed E, Page 181. Indenture April 30, 1810. George Clark

of Fayette County, Kentucky, Jonathan Clark and Richard Cloe Anderson of Jefferson County, Kentucky, to Wm. M. Craig of Shelby County. Refers to deed of trust between George Clark, Jonathan Craig, and Richard C. Anderson by Adam Craig and wife Mary Craig vesting in them George Clark, Jonathan Clark and Richard C. Anderson as trustees to the William M. Craig son of said Adam Craig and Mary a tract of land in Kentucky, set apart for Officers and soldiers of the Virginia, one tract of 1000 acres lying on west fork of Little River, etc. 27 March 1799. etc.

Deeds E, Page 217. Indenture 29 Jany 1821. Squire Van Hooser and Patsy Vanhooser, his wife formerly Patsy Howard, daughter and heir at law of William Howard decd. John Whitesides buys two lots .

Deeds E, Page 231. Edward A. Keeling Admr. of George Keeling decd. VS Charles Robert Dillen, William Purnell, in right of his wife Elissia Purnell formerly Dillen, and Elizabeth Purnell. Elisha Eldirdge and his wife Mary Ann Eldridge formerly Mary Ann Dillon, and George F. Dillen, Thomas D. Dillen, and Edward D. Dillen minor heirs by guardian Elisha Eldridge heirs of Thomas Dillen decd. Suit in court regards lands.

Deed E, Page 248. James Monroe president of the United States of America, Pursuant to Act of Congress, 6 May 1812, George Robertson father of and heir at law of Thomas Robertson (Alias Robertson) deceased, having departed this life; In General Land Office a warrant in his favor No.19346, there is granted to said George Robertson father of and heir of said Thomas Robertson, alias Robertson, decd, late a private in Coventon's Company.

Deeds E, Page 254. August 14, 1818 William Hill and Thomas Hill executors of last will and testament of Thomas Cope, deceased, and Thomas Cope of the other part, made in decree of Chancery and title bond. Signed William x Hill. and Thomas x Hill. Proved Oct. 1820.

Deeds E, Page 268. Power of attorney, John McDonald, David L. Ferrell, and Polly Ferrill, formerly Carlock, who is daughter of Sally Carlock, decd, formerly Sally McDonald, Clement Means, and Nancy Means, formerly Nancy Carlock, daughter of Sally Carlock aforesaid, deceased and Rollins Johnson and Hannah Johnson formerly Hannah Carlock, daughter of Sally Carlock, deceased, formerly Sarah McDonnold, Thomas H. McDonald son of Michael McDonald, deceased, Stokely R. Hill and Polly Hill his wife formerly Polly McDonald, daughter of Michael McDonald, aforesaid, deceased, and Job Carlock guardian for Eley Carlock, Matilda Carlock and Benjamin Laciceu Carlock, infant heirs of aforesaid Sally Carlock decd, and Thomas H. McDonald,guardian of and for the infant heirs of Michael McDonald to wit. Porter McDonald, Patience

McDonald, Nancy McDonald, John McDonald, Sally McDonald, Pheriba McDonald, and Elizabeth McDonald, Jr, children of said Michael McDonald, decd all of Tennessee, Overton County appoints Thomas K. McDonald of County and State as attorney and recover all our several legacies in the County of Limestone, and State of Alabama, both real and personal for property bequeathed or descended to us by our brother and Uncle James McDonnold, decd, formerly of Limestone County, Alabama, etc.

Deeds E, Page 283. Indenture 22 October 1821, John S. Brown, Hawkins Brown, Richard C. S. Brown, Gordon Brown, Jacob Brown, and John F. Sevier heirs of Benjamin Brown, decd, of the County of Overton. 218 acres to Valentine Matlock of said county. All sign.

Deeds E, Page 287. Indenture 24 July 1822. John F. Voss of Spottsylvania County, Virginia, 216 acres to Chatten Chowning of Overton County, Tennessee for and in consideration of the sum of $1000 land in Overton County.

Deeds E, Page 291. Sylvanua Hinds and Joseph Hinds, 352 acres in Overton County, Tennessee, part of the original tract of 4400 acres granted by North Carolina to John Hinds Senr, adjoining Levi Hinds and adjoining Finley. Dec.27, 1817.

Deeds E, Page 294. John McIver to 360 acres Overton County to John Thurman of Cumberland County, Kentucky, land in Overton County, 1820 August 29.

Deeds E, Page 313. Samuel Reno. 23 Sept. 1822. Samuel Reno of McMinn County, Tennessee, to Alexander Davidson of Overton County a tract of land in Overton County on Wolf River.

Deeds E, Page 324. Isaac Van Hooser to Power of Attorney to Abraham VanHooser. Knows all men by these presents, that I, Isaac VanHooser, of the County of Overton and State aforesaid, for divers good causes and consideration me hereunto moving have this day obtained nominated and appointed Abraham V. Hooser my true and lawful attorney, for me in my name and on my behalf and for his use to ask, demand and receive of the Executor or executors, Administrators or legal representatives of Moses Poor, Senior, deceased, all the estate of every sort that I am entitled to in right of my wife hereby ratifying and confirming what my attorney lawfully do or cause to be done allowing him to give and grant such receipts acquittances and discharges as may be necessary in the premises. In testimony whereof I hereunto set my hand and seal this 10th day of October 1820. Signed Isaac (x) Van Hooser. Attest- Adam Huntsman. Stokely R. Hill. Proved in Overton County, 23 April Court.1823.

Deeds E, Page 325. Elizabeth Parrott, Senior of Overton County, for consideration of maternal affection as well as valuable consideration of $500 paid U. S. currency, to me conveys negroes and personal property to Elizabeth Parrott Jr. April 15, 1823.

Deeds E, Page 328. Indenture 1820 William Fleming of Overton County, and Joe Mabry of Warren County, Tenn, 220 acres in Overton County.

Deeds E, Page 329. Indenture 6 March 1820, Jesse Gentry of Todd Co. Ky. deed land in Overton County to James Campbell.

Deeds E, Page 344. Decree. as title. Charles Simmons and Landon Armstrong to Sarah Coe, widow of Giles Coe, decd, et al. Overton Circuit Court Sept. 1823. Heirs of Giles Coe, decd, by their guardian. Sarah Coe widow of Giles Coe and Lucille Coe, infant heir of Giles Coe, decd, by guardian, John Coe, complainant and Charles Simmons and Landon Armstrong and Benj. Totten, Admr. of James McDonnold decd Defendants, Regards land in Overton County, Tenn.

Deeds E, Page 346. 19 April 1823 Stephen Copeland to "Roaring River Baptist Society" Members, three acres forty poles for a Baptist meeting house in Overton County, Tenn.

Deeds E, Page 347. Zebah (Zebediah) Price of Overton County, to John Simpson for to go to Illinois. Power of Attorney, Agreement. Stepson is to go to Illinois, where her husband Nathaniel Price died and where he left before his death some property which I wish him the said Simpson to sell and dispose of as he shall find best and dispose same, etc.
27 July 1823.

Deeds E, Page 350. John B. Cross of Madison County, Tennessee, power of attorney to Maclin Cross, my son to convey slaves in Overton County, Tenn. 15 Sept. 1823.

Deeds E, Page 355. Indenture 27 October 1832. Zebah Price Admrx of Estate of Nathaniel Price, deceased of Overton County, Tennessee, sells 10 acres to John Baskett of Washington County, Tennessee, for $50.00 paid. It being my portion as one of the legatees of my father Jas. Martin whereon my father lived, when he died, adjoining the land of Joseph Bretin and others. Signed Zebah x Price. Proved October 1823.

Deeds E, Page 361. John Miller of McMinn County, 35 acres of land conveys to George Speck, Tract of land Dry Valley near West fork of Obed's River. Dec. 5, 1821.

Deeds E, Page 373. Cornelius Swain 352 acres to Isaac Creselous of Greene County, Tennessee. Land in Overton County. 1818.

Deeds E, Page 385. Indenture April 6, 1819. Nelly Groom as Admrx. for John Groom decd, sells 50 acres land to James Watts of Overton County, Tennessee.

Deeds E, Page 386. Littleton Jenkins heir of Estate of William Jenkins formerly of Overton County, decd, nominates and appoints Nathan Haggard of Sparta White County, Tennessee, to be my attorney to receive from the Estate of William Jenkins decd in my stead. July Court 1824. Overton County.

Deeds E, Page 418. Major James Home, of the Royal Marines, and Helen Homes spouse of George Logan, Esquire, Junr., of Edrom (?) with the special advice of consent of said Geo Logan, my husband and I, said Geo Logan or myself and taking burden on me for my spouse, we both with advice and consent considering that Patrick Hone of Rappahannock forge near Falmouth, Virginia, in North America died lately, as we are informed. James Homes and Helen Homes are brother and sisters, German, of the said deceased Patrick Hones and heirs and next relation to him. Appoint Dr. ---? Vass of Falmouth, Mr. ---? Dunbar of Falmouth and Mr. ---? Patton of Fredericksburg, Virginia, aforesaid appoint attorney. Regards Property 1823.

Deeds E, Page 446. Adam Darby of town of Fredericksburg, in Spottsylvania County, Virginia 1823.

Deeds E, Page 455. 13 Feby 1824. George Price of White County, Tennessee, sells 28 acres of land to Joseph Bartlett of Overton County. Land in Overton County.

Deeds E, Page 467. Indenture 7 Sept. 1825. James Huntsman of Overton County, one part and Adam Huntsman of Madison County and Stephen Huntsman, a minor son of James Huntsman, of third part. Deed trust for negroes, etc.

Deeds E, Page 475. Indenture 4 May 1821. John McIver of Fairfax County, Virginia, to Thomas Elliott of Cumberland County, Kentucky 226 acres of land in Overton County, Tenn.

Deeds E, Page 476. Indenture 29 Sept. 1822. William Baker & Sons of Baltimore Maryland, to Landon Armstrong of Monroe County in Tennessee, 160 acres land in Overton County, Tenn.

Deeds E, Page 507. Indenture 18 July 1821. William Williard, Senr, of Overton County to James Williard his son of same place 130 acres land.

Deeds E, Page 511. Indenture 24 Oct. 1822. William E. Butler of Madison County, Tennessee, and Patsy T. Butler his wife to Abraham Goodpasture and William Williard of Overton County, 49½ acres of land in Overton County.

Deeds E, Page 515. Joel Rice of Madison County, Alabama, to James Chisam of Hardeman County, Tennessee, 500 acres land in Overton County, Tenn. adjoining Russell. 1825.

Deeds E, Page 527. Will of William Armstrong of Overton County, Appoints William Fleming and my son Stephen K. Armstrong my executors to this my last will and testament. To son Hugh C. Armstrong. To son Stephen K. Armstrong. Oct.17, 1817. Proved 1826. recorded in this deed book in Overton Co. Tenn.

Deeds E, Page 533. Chatten Chowning of Overton County, to Barton Philpot of Cumberland County, Kentucky, 216 acres land in Overton County, Tenn. 1825.

Deeds E, Page 534. Ann Quarles of Overton County, bill sale. to James T. Quarles all interest title and claim as a legatee and heir and distributee of my late brother James Howes decd. 23 April 1827.

Deeds E, Page 559. State of Tennessee 16 acres Grant No. 7090 Samuel French 22 April 1820. District 4 Surveyors Office. Founded on certificate No.147. Issued to Edward Scott. Registered East Tennessee to John Brown for 100 acres. 22 August 1810. 16 acres of which are assigned to Samuel French, Tract of land in Overton County and Morgan County, on waters of Crooked Creek, adjoining Pile, etc. including the place and Spring where Joseph French now lives. March 6, 1828.

Deeds E, Page 565. John Tate Sr, of Overton County bill of sale to Robert Tate for love and affection paturnal to lawful son. conveys negroes 1826.

Deeds E, Page 568. John Tate Sr, deed to John and Robert Tate for consideration of paternal love for sons John Jr. and Robert convey tract of land in Overton County. 1826

Deeds E, Page 571. Isaac Holman of Jackson County conveys 163 acres of land to John Stewart. Land in Overton County. 1826

Deeds F, Page 12. Benjamin Totten Sheriff of Jackson County, Tenn. at house of John Bowen esq, in Jackson County where court was held 1803.

Deeds F, Page 12. Indenture 8 May 1828. Benj. Totten of Obion County, Tenn. to James L. Totten of Gibson County, and Benj. C. Totten and Archibald W. O. Totten of Obion County, conveys land in Overton County, Tenn.

Deeds F, Page 17. Charles Smith admr. of Lemmy Davis to Samuel T. Keen. Indenture 23 August 1828. Charles Smith Admr of estate of Stanwicks Hoard decd of Overton County,

Tennessee to Samuel T. Keen. Refers to lot of land No.3. that Lemmy Davis drawed as one of the legatees of estate of said Stanwix Hoard, decd, for consideration of $550 paid by S. F. Keen to Lemmy Davis.

Deeds F, Page 27. Isaac Clendennen of Cumberland County, Kentucky, for and in consideration of $500 sell Jacob Dillon of Overton County certain negroes 1828

Deeds F, Page 38. Thomas Poteet Sr to Thomas Poteet Jr. son the consideration "love and affection" 1829.

Deeds F, Page 38. Dec. 18, 1827. John Reamy sells land to Pleasant Poteet where Reamy now lives.

Deeds F, Page 39. Thomas Poteet Sen. bill of sale to Mills Poteet, for "love and affection for daughter". gives negro girl. 1827

Deeds F, Page 49. James Cargile Senr bill of sale to James Cargile Jr. for "Fatherly and paternal affection" conveys negro girl 1829.

Deeds F, Page 60. Will of Henry Reagan of Overton County, Tenn. 8 Sept. 1829. Sound mind and memory. My oldest son John Reagan, saddle, bridle and what I have already given him. My daughter Mary Poore one negro named Jacob now in her possession. My daughter Lavinia Reagan one negro named Rose and etc. To my son Charles Reagan a negro named Kitty and etc. Land I now live on. My son William Reagan negro and land. Refers to all the books he now has equally divided between his children. Appoints son Charles Reagan executor. Witness. Wm. Chilton Jr. A. L. Barmblett. Joseph Poore. Proved October 1829.

Deeds F, Page 67. John Taylor and Frances Taylor of Hanover County, Virginia, for "love and affection to Edmund J. Taylor", all right and interest in Estate of James Haws late of Overton County, Tenn. decd. August 8, 1829. Proved Hanover County, Virginia.

Deeds F, Page 93. Cornelius Carmack, Senr, deed to Wm. Carmack his son "natural love and affection" Tract of land on which said William now lives. 22 Jany 1830.

Deeds F, Page 113. Ann Quarles of Overton County, for "love and affection to Granddaughter Ann Huntsman" and $1.00 deeds slaves. 1830. Signed Ann (x) Quarles. James T. Quarles.

Deeds F, Page 127. Will of Michaek Hickey of Overton County. I gave to Middleton Hickey one horse and etc. I gave to Banister Hickey one horse,I gave to Martha Hickey one horse. I gave to John Hickey one colt, etc. I give to Mary Hickey horse, etc. I give to Joshua Hickey horse and saddle etc.

I gave to James Hickey horse, etc. I gave to Michael Hickey Junr, horse etc. Household goods and land I live on to wife her life and at her death divided. Middleton my eldest son to live on the place and care for his mother. Son Middleton and James Turner executors. 22 March 1824.

Deeds F, Page 133. William Hoard of Madison County, Tenn, letters of attorney to Wm. Donaldson, 20 Sept. 1830.

Deeds F, Page 147. Indenture 13 August 1829. Rhoda Collier of Franklin County, to Enoch Murphree of Overton County, conveys 50 acres in Overton County.

Deeds F, Page 147. Indenture 9 Sept. 1830. Isaac Fansher and Benum Fancher of Clark County, Illinois. John Myler and wife Patsy of Myler County, Illinois and James and Alexander Fancher of Overton County, in Tennessee. Consideration $500 all interest and claim as heir of Richard Fancher, decd of Overton County, Tenn.

Deeds F, Page 153. Will of Henry H. Atkinson of Overton County, Tenn. wife Sally. My children except my child Lucinda Evans or the child I legitamated by order of County Court. land in Fentress County. Appoints my brother William Atkinson and Jacob Dillon my executors. 16 August 1830. Proved Oct. 1830.

Deeds F, Page 153. Indenture April 13, 1829 Coleby and Susannah Creed his wife of Overton County, sell 148 acres land to James McMillen.

Deeds F, Page 154. Indenture 18 Oct. 1830. John Harris of Cooper Co. Mo. sells 75 acres to John Holsell of Overton County, Tenn.

Deeds F, Page 160. Indenture 17 May 1830. Between Benjamin Walker of Overton County and John L. Copeland, Eliza Copeland, James C. Chaney, Nancy Chaney, Henry B. Smith, Priscilla Smith, William Seahorn and Catharine Seahorn. for $802. paid by Benjamin Walker, 106¾ acres of land in Overton County.

Deeds F, Page 169. Indenture Oct. 1, 1829. William Whitlow of Clarke County, Georgia to Thomas Maxwell of Overton County, Tenn. 60 acres in Overton County.

Deeds F, Page 181. Henry Dillon and James Willard admrs of Wm. Dillon decd 100 acres on waters Roaring River to Edmund Brewer, Oct. 1, 1827.

Deeds F, Page 183. Indenture 17 March 1827 James Officer of White County, Tennessee, to Wm. Cheney (might be Cherry ?) 124 acres waters of West fork.

Deeds F, Page 186. Will of Charles Matlock of Overton County, Tennessee, wife Elizabeth one third of personal estate for life. To my children. Son Overton. Daughter Alia, Daughter Melinda, Daughter Menervia, Daughter Mary Nelson, and Daughter Analiza. Wife pregnant with child. Appoints my brother Moore Matlock executor. April 9, 1819. Witness Jobe Carlock. Adam Winningham. Robt. L. Ferril. Proved April 1819. Overton County.

Deeds F, Page 191. Indenture 23 August 1830. Joseph Copeland of Overton County, Tennessee, to Benjamin Taynes of Wayne County, Kentucky, for $500 paid. 150¾ acres of land on waters of Roaring River in Overton County, Tennessee.

Deeds F, Page 198. Indenture 16 March 1810 Charles Simmons of Washington County, Miss., to Jesse Scott of Overton County, Tennessee 169 acres land on bank of Cumberland River.

Deeds F, Page 210. Indenture 20 July 1826. John Johnston of Hardeman County, Tennessee, 200 acres land in three tracts to Joseph Bartlett of Overton County.

Deeds F, Page 215. James W. Clarke by his attorney William Snodgrass sells 100 acres of land on Bear Creek to Jesse Stewart.

Deeds F, Page 218. Refers to Loyd Morgan of Jackson County, Tenn., 10 acres in Overton County, 1828.

Deeds F, Page 219. Indenture 18 December 1827. Jane Webb, John Webb, Thomas Webb, James Webb, Elizabeth Webb, Hubbard Johnson of Overton County, Tenn, and James Hooten, Jesse Brown, and Reubin Mart of Ashe County, North Carolina, of one part to John Johnson of Overton County, Tennessee, for and in consideration $1353, paid by John Johnson conveys 570 acres land on Spring Creek in two tracts Grant No.384 and 2797. All sign.

Deeds F, Page 226. Refers to Gideon Harris of Maddison Co. Tenn.

Deeds F, Page 228. Will of James (x) Cargile of Overton County of advanced in life, infirmaties incident to age. To son Lewis Cargile, To son James Cargile, to son John Cargile, to Son Charles Cargile, to son Jonathan Cargile. Son-in-law Isaac Crouch. Son in law William Smeddy (or Snoddy ?), Wife Magdaline. Appoints Jacob Dillon executor. June 7, 1830. Signed James (x) Cargile. Witneses- J. H. Dillon, A. R. Storey, J. Dillon, Jesse Hull. Proved 1831 May 25.

Deeds F, Page 231. Indenture January 1, 1828. Lenard Davis of Overton County to Jonathan Davis, Jacob Davis, Thomas

Davis, Lem'l Davis, Matthew Davis, Isaac Davis, Wm. Davis, Jonathan Roberts, Hugh Roberts, and John Stone of other part. for $10.00 conveys 14 slaves. All those named being sons and sons-in-law and for good will and affection. Also conveys 440 acres of land. Signed Leonard Davis.

Deeds F, Page 239. Indenture 5 Sept. 1830 Isaac Johns of one part and Ezekiel Grissum of other part, conveys 100 acres of land on Roaring River. Signed by Isaac Johns.

Deeds F, Page 239. Samuel McCraw of Overton County, now old and far advanced in life and having an "affectionate feeling for my daughter Elenor McCraw" and for her welfare, Knowing my life is short, give unto my daughter aforesaid three tracts of land on Obed's River 115 acres 4 negroes and other property Tract land I now live on in Overton County.

Deeds F, Page 245. State of Tennessee Grant No.2874. 125 acres land on waters Eagle Creek. 1823 by No.235. Granted by Tennessee unto Daniel L. Windle, Robert S. Windle and Samuel W. Windle. 1835

Deeds F, Page 247. John Johnston bill of sale to Margaret Johnston for "love and affection to daughter". and $1.00 paid conveys slaves and etc. April 23 1831

Deeds F, Page 248. William Upton, conveys 50 acres to his daughter Nancy Upton. consideration being "natural love and affection". April 1, 1823.

Deeds F, Page 249. Indenture June 14, 1831. Peterson Cherry late of Illinois, by his attorney in fact James McDonald of Overton County, Tennessee, to Robert L. Ferril, William Hayter, and John McDonald of Overton County, Tennessee, conveys 2 acres land on Camp Ground for Presbyterian Church and promoting love of God. for Meeting House on waters Nettle Carrier Creek, in Overton County.

Deeds F, Page 250. Indenture 17 Sept. 1831. John Reagan of Territory of Arkansas. 118 acres in Overton County, Tennessee, to James Amonett of Overton County.

Deeds F, Page 252. Daniel Graham, admrx, of estate of John McIver deceased makes conveyances in 1831.

Deeds F, Page 256. Mitchell Terry and wife Nancy of Jackson County, Tennessee, sell 50 acres in Overton County by Josiah Copeland. 1831.

Deeds F, Page 259. Indenture 19 Sept. 1831. John McDonnold of one part, sells 228 acres on Sandy River to William Fleming of Weakley County, Tennessee.

Deeds F, Page 258. Refers to Wm. Fleming of Weakley County,

Tennessee.

Deeds F, Page 261. Andrew I. Marchbanks of McMinnville, Warren County, Tennessee, sold negro Andy to Jacob Dillon for $450. 23 Sept. 1831.

Deeds F, Page 261. Adam Huntsman for $350 paid by virtue of being admr. of James Huntsman decd, sells negro Melinda to Valentine Matlock. 23 Jany 1826.

Deeds F, Page 271. 24 Decr. 1831. James McDonnold Admr. of Estate of Redmund McDonnold decd late of Fentress Co., Tenn. to Wm. Chilton of said County for $560 paid, conveys slaves.

Deeds F, Page 275. John Holford, Senr, 49¼ acres land on waters Spring Creek held by grant conveys to son Matthew Holford of said county for love and affection. Jany 4,1832.

Deeds F, Page 273. Indenture Feb. 1, 1832. Moses Fisk of Overton County to John Rennow of Cumberland County, Kentucky 2010 acres held by grant, on Wolf River in Overton County, Tennessee.

Deeds F, Page 275. William Douglass of Knox County, Tennessee, for "love and good will and affection to my two sons", Thomas Douglass and William Douglass Jr. land in Overton County.

Deeds F, Page 285. April 6, 1832. John Renneau of Cumberland County, Kentucky, sells to Stephen Seeval (Sewal ?) of Overton County, 200 acres land in Overton County, Tenn. 1832

Deeds F, Page 286. April 26, 1832 John Reneau of Cumberland County, Kentucky, to Polly Griffin the lawful infant heir of William Griffin decd and for $75.00 paid all claim against said Griffin estate.

Deeds F, Page 288. Nov. 4, 1830. Martha Stone Admrx James Stone, and Jeremiah Stone, Admrs, of last will and testament of Micajah Stone decd of Overton County convey to Usebias Stone for consideration $416 paid, 40¾ acres of land in Overton County, All sign.

Deeds F, Page 289. Refers to a conveyance of Richard Stone, consideration being $795. Seems to refer to the same as on page 288.

Deeds F, Page 296. 16 May 1832 Reuben Carlock of McLean County, Illinois, to Jefferson Goodpasture of Overton County, 85 acres land on Roaring River in Overton County, Tennessee.

Deeds F, Page 297. December 7, 1830 John Love of Green Co. Tennessee conveys 100 acres to James Riley of Overton County.

Deeds F, Page 298. Josiah Brown deeds 50 acres on waters Roaring River to Samuel Brown of Overton County. all his interest in land in Overton County, Josiah Brown of McLean County, Illinois. 22 Sept. 1831.

Deeds F, Page 301. 20 April 1832. John Coe and Nancy Coe, his wife late Nancy Scott of Cumberland County, Kentucky. John Kerr and Sally his wife late Salley Scott, William Barry and Frances his wife late Frances Scott, Thomas T. Halsell and Rebecca his wife formerly Rebecca Scott, and Benjamin Sims and Patsey his wife late Patsy Scott, heirs and representatives of Jesse Scott, decd, of Monroe County, Kentucky, sell John Sims of Overton County, Tennessee, 163 acres land in Overton County. All sign.

Deeds F, Page 310. John Renneau of Cumberland County, Kentucky, to Isaac T. and Joseph W. Renneau for $4000, sells and conveys 400 acres land in Overton County, Tennessee on the Kentucky line.

Deeds F, Page 314. October court 1816. William A Turner, Thomas Turner, James W. Clark, the heirs of Thomas Thompson, decd by their guardian John Jones and James Chisum, petition to distribute shares in land.

Deeds F, Page 317. Thomas and William Turner heirs of Daniel Turner decd referred to.

Deeds F, Page 317. State of Bullock County, in Georgia --- We the heirs of Alisha Turner late of Bullock County, Georgia, appoint Benj. Turner one of the heirs of said Alisha Turner, as attorney to act in our stead in the estate matters. Estate of his brother Thomas Turner decd of Overton County, Tennessee. Signed by Thomas (x) Turner, Arthur Turner, John Turner, James Turner, Judson Alwood, Isaac Turner.

Deeds Q, Page 58. Ruth Martin lease deed 150 acres on Obed's River to R. H. Hall. Agreement, Ruth Martin and J. B. Martin of first part and R. B. Hall, for consideration of $1.00 and $50. paid when any oil or valuable minerals are obtained which is hereby acknowledged. The first party agrees to let the party of the second part drill on land in Overton County on south side Obed's River below the mouth of Mitchell Creek, on 100 acre tract and land on which J. B. Martin now lives. Adjoining on north by said River on west by Nancy Smith land and on south by Z. R. Chowning land and on the east by J. Rileys the part of the second part refers to Mitchell Creek 50 acres adjoining the lands of Aaron Stinson, A. Garrett widow Pierce etc. 29 March 1865.

Deeds N, Page 591. Creed T. Huddleston deed 200 acres District No.12 on waters of etc. etc. to Wiley H. Huddleston. Whereas hertofore on 7th November 1848 Creed T. Huddleston late of Overton County, executed to Wiley Huddleston of said

County a certain title bond of that date thereby the said Creed T. Huddleston bargained and sold said Wiley H. Huddleston for the consideration of $100 a certificate tract of land in said county 200 acres including a place known as the Rich flat excepting some 300 acres of same with the place on which Jno. Harris once lived and known by the name of Harrises old place. Winburn W. Goodpasture was appointed and qualified administrator De bonus nou of said estate and is now duly acting as such Admr. Now therefore in consideration of the premises said Goodpasture as such Admr. De bonus now for and in behalf of said Estate do hereby transfer and convey to the said W. V. Huddleston and his heirs forever the said tract of land etc. 6 October 1857. Signed W. W. Goodpasture. Proved Overton County, Oct. 6, 1857.

Deeds N, Page 201. Wiley Huddleston deed tract of land held by Grant No.300 lying in the County of Overton on waters of Wolf River to J. A. and W. C. Huddleston 19 Dec. 1855. Indenture made and entered into this 19th day of December in the year of our Lord one thousand eight hundred and fifty five by and between J. A. Huddleston, W. C. Huddleston of the one part and Wiley Huddleston and Willis Huddleston and John Huddleston, Thomas S. Huddleston, Joseph Combs and Lucy A. Combs, and Green B. Murphey and Charlotte his wife of Fentress County, Tennessee and part of Overton County. Whereas Huddleston, Combs and Murphey have sold unto J. A. and W. C. Huddleston for $30 each, paid, acknowledged, all their rite and interest to a certain piece of land lying in Overton County on waters of Wolf River, adjoining John Graham, to Simon H. Huddleston line, etc. thereunto belonging and being all the estate right interest that Wiley H. Huddleston, Willis Huddleston, John B. Huddleston, Thomas S. Huddleston, Joseph Combs and Lucy his wife, and Green B. Murphey and his wife Charlotte, have to the said land premises, unto J. A. Huddleston and William C. Huddleston their heirs and assigns forever. W. H. Huddleston and Willis Huddleston and John B. Huddleston and Thomas S. Huddleston, Joseph Combs, etc etc. etc. all sign. Attest - Willey H. Huddleston. Willis H. Huddleston. Proved 18 March 1856.

Deeds K, Page 252. John Richardson conveys to Abram Carr, Benjamin Carr, Thomas Carr, Junr, William Marius, John Carmack and Richard Copeland and their heirs forever for the use of the neighborhood and for a $1.00 consideration a lot in Dist. No.6. containing one acre. Adjoins Chappins line, signed John Richardson 30 Nov. 1846.

Deeds J, Page 202. Abraham Weaver by his will to John Richison. Indenture 20 July 1842. Abraham Weaver of Madison County, Tenn., to John Richardson of Overton County, Abraham Weaver for and in consideration of $14.00 paid conveys to John Richardson and his heirs a tract of land 8 acres by survey in said Overton County on Roaring River including the part of John Bodley's improvement in Roaring River, Signed Abraham Weaver by C. Weaver his lawful attorney.

Deeds A, Page 81. Overton County, 1798. James Mebane, Grant No.378 from North Carolina 5000 acres granted includes improvement of Franklin, Robbins and Huddleston. Dec. 27, 1800.

Andrew Jackson owned two tracts of land on West fork, May 29, 1806. recorded in Overton County, Book A page 162.

David Mebane, Executor of James Mebane, decd. power of attorney to Henry Reagan to sell 5000 acres on Wolf and Obed's River Oct. 1807. Book A page 232.

Grant No.379 to James Mebane Jr, for 500 acres adjoining or near the Indian boundary, on Eagle Creek, waters of Obed's River. Dec. 27, 1800. (Tenn. Land Office).

Thomas and Robert King 1000 acres in Middle District on a branch of Wolf River joining survey to include Salt Lick etc. July 10, 1788. Samuel Johnson, Governor, Book 4. (Land Office, Nash.)

Thomas and Robert King 5000 acres on Spring Creek four miles from Salt Lick. Grant No.53. (Book A, page 27). July 10, 1788, Surveyed by Stockley Donelson, Robert King and Alexander Blair, chain carrier. (Land Office, Nash.).

North Carolina Grant No.162. to Henry Conway for 640 acres land begins "where the new road to the Cumberland was missed by the pilots" at a place called "the barrens" 1790 (Land Office, Nash.)

Grant No.380 to Samuel Scott for 500 acres on Wolf River, Beginning on the mouth of a Big Cave Spring South 640 E.1280 N 640 W 1280. H. Rowan, Surveyor, John Latham and Wm. McCormack, chain Carrier. (Land Office Nashville.)

Grant No.382. to Micajah Thomas 1000 acres. Wolf River on Lick and Yoacum Creek, joining Polks 500 acre tract where John McDonald now lives, and Felps Reed grant. Sept. 15, 1801. H. Rowan surveyor. Jacob Howe and Wm. Livingston, chain carrier. (Land Office Nashville).

Grant No.199 to John Hinds and Francis Mayberry 4000 acres on Wolf River. Begins on South Bank near mouth of a spring branch above where an old path crosses the river, opposite some small island. June 24, 1793. Stockley Donelson. Surveyor. James Cunningham and Francis Latham, chain carriers.

Grant No.71 to Robert and Thomas King for 2000 acres begins at a place known as Banks on Wolf River. Both sides of path that leads from the mouth of the Holston to the Ford of Wolf

River, July 10, 1788. Samuel Johnson, Governor. Robert King and George Fields, chain carrier. (Land office, Nash.)

Grant No.307 to John Geddy 500 acres on a fork of Obed. Begins on an oak and black locust on the Kentucky line. March 7, 1796. Samuel Ashe, Governor. Stockley Donelson, surveyor. Leon Bradley and John Lyons, chain carriers. (Land Office, Nashville.)

Grant No.300 to John Sevier Sr. 32000 acres. Begins on Southeast corner of 25000 acre survey, Nov. 27. 1795. George Gordon, Surveyor. Joseph Sevier, Phillip Lovelady, chain carriers. (Note - According to A. R. Hogue, this includes the eastern part of Overton and nearly all of Pickett County.)

Grant No.228 to John Sevier. Land adjoins Stockley Donelson, 25060 acres in County of Sumner on waters of Cumberland River. Dated 1795. (Note - A. R. Hogue says, This covers parts of Overton, Pickett and Fentress Counties, extends to near Pall Mall on Wolf River in Fentress County. This seems to be one of the grants of land upon which charges of fraud were made against Sevier, mentioned in "McGee's History of Tennessee".)

Grant No.367. Archibald Lyttle. 300 acres on Obeds River, Jany 23, 1800. The chain carriers were Jason Thompson and Oliver Williams. The surveyor was S. Williams. (Note - Lyttle was one of the agents for laying off the lands granted the Continental line.)

Grant No.369, to Felps Reed, 3000 acres on both sides of Lick Creek of Wolf River, the sugar tree forest, including two improvements, Griggs and Goodens. Feb. 18, 1800.

North Carolina Grant Book 4 (Tennessee Land Office, Nashville.) Thomas and Robert King 1000 acres on a branch of Wolf River Begins at Southeast corner from Salt Lick joining a survey to include a Salt Lick. July 10, 1788.

North Carolina Grant No.380. To Samuel Scott, Continental Line 1800, land on Wolf River, Begins at mouth of Cane Spring.This seems to be the same land deeded to Simon Huddleston by Scott in 1804. Henry Reagan and Wiley Huddleston are witnesses. (Book K deeds page 22 Overton Co.)

Grant No.372 to William Polk 500 acres on Wolf River including McConnel's improvement. On South side of Lick Creek. April 17, 1800. (Book A page 246.)

Grant No.373 to William Polk, 640 acres on south side on Obed on both sides of a wagon road cut by George Gordon from the Old Cumberland Trace to Wolf River passing Captain Thomas Elliott's plantation. Entered April 30, 1784. Dated

May 26, 1800. B. Williams, Governor of N. C.

Grant No.374 to William Polk, heir of Thomas Polk. 1784. North Carolina grant.

INFORMATION

The following records are available in Fentress County Courthouse:

Deeds from 1823

Wills from 1904

Marriages from 1904

Circuit Court Clerk's Office Docket Books begin 1872

Clerk and Master's Docket Books begin about 1870

All other early records destroyed.

E.R.W.

LEGISLATIVE PETITION 1801-1860

On file in the Tennessee State Archives, Nashville, are many original papers, among which are to be found various petitions relative to matters of interest and to people of Overton and those counties carved from Overton. These petitions often carry long lists of signatures (original signatures) of those persons living in the county. They are filed according to years, along with other counties in Tennessee, and I here give those for Overton, Fentress, Putman, and the area of interest for this publication.... Some of these petitions give vital genealogical information.

E. R. W.

1813. Overton County, Petition of Stephen Copeland regards a turnpike.

1813. Overton County, Petition of Denson Fields for divorce.

1815. Overton County, Regards tobacco inspection in said county.

1815. Overton County, Petition regarding pay for guns impressed during Creek War.

1815. Overton County, Petition about a bridge over Obed River.

1815. Overton County, Conrad Pyle (Pile) asking that tolls be collected on the turnpike road from Poplar Creek to Wolf River.

1815. Overton County, Benjamin Totten and John McDonald, for land warrant of 300 acres.

1813. Overton County, Benjamin Totten and Jno. McDaniel(?) relative to land grants in Overton County.

1806. Overton County, Stephen Copeland and Daniel McDaniel, et al carrying an Indian to Jail.

1815. Election Certificates for members of the Legislature from Overton County.

1815. Election of Justices of Peace, for Overton County, includes Captains and acting Justices.

1817. Election certificates for members of the Legislature from Overton County. Also for Justices of the Peace.

1817. Petition for New Road. Overton County.

1817. Petition of Ira Sutherland and McGraw regards a road -- Overton County.

1817. Petitions from citizens of Overton, White and Jackson Counties, regards road. (Several different petitions and signed by many, many people.)

1819. Petition from Overton County relating to Jno. Lilly and his citizenship.

1819. Election Reports for Governor and Constitution. Overton County.

1821. Overton County -- Cumberland Turnpike Company, toll gate -- David Thomas, release of fine, etc.

1823. Overton County, Petition to reduce the size of the County. Provides for survey of county.

1823. Legislative election returns for Overton County.

1824. Petition of Henry W. Francus, election and courts of Fentress County. Also a Petition of John Long regarding lands. (both in same pack)

1824. Petition of Henry Rowen relative to land. Overton County.

1824. Petition of William Stewart from Overton County, asking to be granted a divorce.

1824. Overton County, Petition regarding County line and County seat.

1825. Fentress County, James Payne asking for speedy trial.

1825. Overton County. Petition of Charles Matlock regarding lands.

1825. Overton County, William Chilton land. 32000 acres by Jno. Sevier.

1825. Overton County, Will Hills land.

1825. Overton County. Relief of Jno. Harris clerk

1825. Overton County. Adam Gardenhire, release as bail

1825. Overton County, Land of Wm. Armstrong.

1825. Overton County, Stephen Copeland, liquor, to sell without license.

1825. Overton County. Regards Robert Jackson's land.

1825. Overton County. James Bates, resignation as Turnpike Commissioner.

1825. Election Returns for Governor and State Senate for Overton County.

1825. Report of Captain's Companies and Justices of the Peace for Overton and Fentress Counties.

1826. Overton County, Petition of Thomas McBath asks relief.

1826. Overton County, William Rhea regards juror's fees

1826. Overton County, Albert Townsend seeking divorce

1826. Overton County, Elizabeth Dennis, seeking divorce

1826. Certificates of election, Justices of Peace and Captains of Companies, Fentress County.

1827. Overton County, William Evans gun impressed (Indian War 1814-1815).

1827. Overton County, Thomas Simpson regards registration of deeds.

1827. Certificates of election. House of Representatives and Constitutional Convention. Fentress and Overton Counties.

1827. Certificates Captain Companies and Justices of Peace, for Overton and Fentress Counties.

1829. Overton County, S. Dixon for divorce.

1829. Overton County. Joshua Garland to change name.

1829. Fentress County, John Pile asking for divorce.

1829. Fentress County, Petition to be attached to Overton County --- change county line.

1831. Fentress County, Navigation of Obed River.

1831. Fentress County, Relating to muster in the county.

1831. Overton County, Rebecca Ashburn seeking divorce.

1831. Overton County, Michael C. Cole seeking divorce.

1831. Overton County, G. Hawkins release from prosecution.

1831. Overton County, Pertains to county line.

1831. Overton County, Thomas Conway asking for divorce.

1831. Overton County, No tax on town lots.

1831. Overton County, Michael Hall seeking divorce.

1831. Overton County, Benjamin Brown asking to be allowed to peddle without license.

1831. Overton County, List of Captains Companies, and Justices of the Peace.

1831. Overton County, Robert Paige, claim for gun impressed in Creek War.

1831. Report of clerks, Criminal Court, date of dockets, 1824-1829 inclusive. Overton County.

1832. Overton County, E. Walker asking for divorce.

1832. Overton County, Samuel Walker asking for divorce.

1833. Fentress County, George Gordon et al turnpike road

1833. Fentress County, John Wylan, compensation for services

1833. Fentress County, Regards turnpike, petition.

1833. Fentress County, Wolf River navigation.

1833. Fentress County, J. N. Clemmons, compensation

1833. Fentress County, W. Crockett et al. release from judgment.

1833. Credentials of members of House and Senate, General Assembly of Tennessee. Election returns Overton and Fentress Counties.

1835. Wolf Scalps bounties, various counties include Overton, etc.

1835. Election certificates of Senate, Justices of the Peace, Governor, etc. Fentress and Overton Counties.

1835. Circuit Court Clerks. and Co. Court Clerks. Report on Taxes. Fentress and Overton Counties.

1837. Election certificates. Fentress and Overton Counties.

1839. Fentress County. C. Frogge, release from forfeitures.

1839. Overton County, White County and Jackson County for a new county.

1823. Fentress and Overton Counties, Petition in regard to County line.

1833. Overton County, Ambrose Gore to be released from fine.

1833. Overton County, Jno. Gardenshire to be released from forfeited bond.

1833. Fentress County, Jno. Wright asking to sell liquor without license.

1835. Fentress County, Petition of the subject of turnpike road.

1852. Fentress County, Asking for turnpike charter to Robt. Boles.

1825. John M. Clemons, Circuit Court Clerk. Fentress County.

1830. G. W. Sevier, Circuit Clerk. Overton County.

1832. Bond, E. N. Cullom. Clerk of Overton County.

1843. Fentress County, Asking the establishment of a separate court to be held at the Van Buren Academy house.

1843. Overton County, Change County line -- refers to the Walton Road.

1832. Overton County, Geo. Wallace, to hawk and peddle.

No date. Fentress County, Solomon W. Jones asked to be allowed to hawk and peddle.

No date. Overton County. Asks for lottery for the purpose of cleaning out obstructions in Obed River and building a bridge over same.

No date. Moses Fisk asks to open road from his place at Hilham toward Burksville, Kentucky.

No date. For Tennessee Road over Cumberland Mountain to Jesse Savage.

1845. Fentress County, Mathew W. Wright asks to erect a mill and slope dam across Obed's River near the mouth of Crab Creek.

1845. Fentress County, Asks for law against grazing.

1845. Fentress & Overton Counties. Jonathan D. Hale and

Jno. F. Jonett, ask to erect a saw and grist mill on Wolf River at a place known as the Old Huddleston place.

1845. Overton County, Asking the change to be made in the roads from Livingston to Albany.

1826. Misc. petitions from Overton County. (a bunch of them)

1813. Election Returns, Overton County.

1865-66 Overton County, G. W. Overstreet, representative, certificate of election.

1847. Fentress County. For and against Scott's Turnpike Road.

1847. Fentress County, Joshua Wright asking that a charter be granted to build a turnpike road intersecting Scott's Road.

1847. Fentress County, Wade H. Erwin asking to be allowed to operate a grocery store without license.

1847. Fentress County. O. H. Dobkins and others asking to charter road Montgomery to the Bark turnpike.

1847. Fentress County. Asking that an attorney be appointed for each county in this State.

1847. Jackson County, asking that a portion of Jackson County be attached to the County of Overton.

1851. Fentress County, Asking relief of the heirs of Jno. Barton decd, former trustee.

1851. Jackson, White and Overton Counties, asking that a new County be organized.

1843. Overton County, Petition asking change county line, refers to the Walton Road.

1855. Overton County, asking for an additional Justice of the Peace.

1859. Fentress County. Mathis Baker and Matthew Frost for re-imbursement of money and time spent in search of the murders of a man (found by them, lying in the woods on Cumberland Mountain) Palcal and Phillip Mann having been found guilty of murder of said man (gives no name) Palcal (Pascal ?) brought to Justice. Phillip escaped.

1859. Overton County, John L. Hamilton asking compensation in re-case of the State of Tennessee VS Jeremiah Baker and Pascal Mann for the murder of John Fugate.

1859. Overton County, Asking the removal of the Branch Bank of Tennesse at Sparta to Livingston.

1857. Fentress County, Asking the removal of the County seat.

1857. Fentress County, Asking for amendment to the charter to the Montgomery turnpike road.

1857. Fentress County, Petition of S. C. Moore for the benefit of Pleasant Taylor of said county.

1861. Fentress County, Asking a change in the County line.

1861. Fentress County, Asking release of the securities of Jeremiah Hood, tax collector for Fentress County.

1861. Putman County, Asking change in County line.

1841. Fentress County, Asking that Jesse Wood be allowed to sell spiritous liquors without tax.

1841. Fentress County, Asking that Samuel Scott the owner of a turnpike road be required to erect a bridge over Clear Fork and Emory River.

1841. Jackson, Overton, Fentress and White Counties, Asking a new County to be established to be called Putman.

1841. Morgan County, David Smith asking a charter to be granted to him for a turnpike road leading from Jamestown to Montgomery.

1842. Overton County, Asks relief from banking and laws of execution.

1842. Report of the Committee on the bill to establish the County of Putman (contains statements of S. Douglas as to survey of Overton in 1832).

1843. Election reports various counties, include Overton, Fentress, etc.

1851. Overton County, Protesting against the division of the Academy funds.

1851. Putman County, Report of the Judiciary Commission in the case of said county.

1853. Fentress County, James J. Richardson elected Justice of Peace for said county.

1853. Overton County, Fentress County, Morgan and Scott Counties -- Josiah S. Copeland, John Bowles and Allen McDonald.

1853. Fentress County, Certificates of election, William C. Wood, B. L. Staples, and William Pile.

1853. Overton County, certificate of election, Bennie G. Chowning, Henry W. Colgnett, Willis Holliford, Winburm Goodpasture.

1857. Certificate of election. Overton, Morgan, Fentress and Scott Counties. Jefferson D. Goodpasture and J. Bowles.

1857. Certificate of election Legislators. Overton County, James R. Copeland, Burrel G. Chowning, Wm. E. B. Jones. Robert S. Windle and John Hamelton.

LEGISLATIVE PETITION, OVERTON COUNTY, TENNESSEE 1813

On the back, H. Reprs. Oct.26th, 1813. Read and sent to Senate. A. Wilson, clerk.

Senate, Oct. 27th, 1813. Laid on the table. T. J. Campbell.

To the Honourable The General Assembly of the State of Tennessee now in Session ....

The Petition of the subscribers, Inhabitants of the County of Overton, Humbly Sheweth, that they here Disposed. To have a part in the Present War with Britanie Majesty's Savage Allies, Viz. The Creek Nation of Indians, and conceiving they can Render Greater Services To The United States, as Mounted men than they could possibly do on foot, do Humbly Request That Your Honourable Body Would pass a law authorizing, Colonal Stephen Copeland of Said County to Raise by Voluntary Inlistment a force of 500 Mounted men out of the 3d Judicial Circuit In Said State To March against the said Nation of Indians or other Tribes of the savage foe, and fight Them in theire wodn savage way, and act as Rangers & c, so long as it May appear necessary and that the said Volunteer Force When so Raised may be paid and allowed the same pay for theire services as other mounted men are allowed. In the services of the United States on Similar occasions. And that the Senators and Representatives in the Congress of the United States Be instructed to Cause the said Act when passed by your Honourable body to be sanctioned by the National Legislature & c.

An your Petitioners shall ever pray & c.

1. B. Totten
2. Jas. W. Campbell
3. Moore Matlock
4. James Finley
5. Wilie Hudleston
6. Thos Livingston
7. John Hackton (?)
8. ----?----
47. Samuel Denton
48. William Upton
49. Peter Arnet
50. Jessee Ashburn
51. William Upton
52. William McConney
53. John Horn
89. Joel Paris
90. David Stuart
91. Jon. H. Windle
92. Wm. Every
93. Isaiah Ruckman
95. Solomon Alrid
96. Isaac Hoover
97. Britten Smith
98. James Parks
1. B. Totten
2. Jas. W. Campbell
3. Moore Matlock
4. James Finley
5. Wilie Hudleston
6. Thos Levingston
7. John Heckton
8. Robt. Adkinson
9. John Meller
10. Phillip Wherey (?)
11. Arthur Mitchel
12. Isaick ---- ?
13. Benjn. Parrott
14. Saml. Miller
15. Thos. Burford
16. Joseph Campbell

94. William Alrid
18. John Bughes(Hughes ?)
19. Wm. Fleming
20. Benjn Brown
21. Jos. Harriss
22. Jno. Kennedy
23. Eliga rogers
24. John SIsco
25. Michel Speer
26. r. Nels
27. James Boser(?)
28. --- ? ---
---. ~~James~~ Johnson(?)
47. Samuel Denton(?)
48. William Upton
49. Peter Arnet
50. Jessee Ashburn
51. William Upton
52. William McConney
53. John Horn(?)
54. John Walker
55. Corneles Carmack
56. Thomas McDaniel(?)
57. Severn Alley (Levern ?)
58. Joseph Eoney(?)
59. William Boswell
60. James Lee
61. James Offner
62. Filip Upton
63. Thomas Jenny (Jennings ?)
64. Guillow Sams(?)
65. Jacob Davis
66. William Simpson
67. Hollel Herron
68. Cornelas Connedy
69. Isaac Hooser
70. Edmon Crafford
71. William Stoutt
72. Henning Gore
73. Isa Row(?)
74. John Lee
75. Robert Sevsis(?)
89. Joel Paris
90. David Stuart
91. Jon H. Windle
92. Wm. Evans
93. Isaiah Ruckman
94. Wm. Alrid
95. Solomon Alrid
96. Isaac W. (?) (Hooser)
97. Britton Smith
98. James Parks
99. Joshua Morrison
17. Arthur Babb
100. Saml. Callahan
101. Francis Chany
102. Alexr. Henslee
103. Chas. Matney
104. James Key
105. Abrm. Fulfer(?)
106. Wm. Cooksey
107. Pattn. Pool
108. Ephraim Wykoff
109. John Workman
110. Benjn. Workman
111. Robert Dale
112. Peter Bilyeu(Bilyew ?)
113. John Maxwell
114. Hardy Honeycutt
115. James Maxwell
116. Isaac Cuningham
117. Jessy Gentry
118. Thos Gallion
119. Wm. Dale

The above names were wrote by me Jo. H. Windle at a Genl. Muster by their requests.

Mason Kelly

Page 3 of the original petition

Elijah Rogers

28. James Smith
29. Stephen Horn
30. Saml. Brown
31. Jacob Swallow
32. Zacriah Eldridge
33. John Hamoc (NOTE: There was a Hammock family in the Co. ERW)
34. William Copeland
35. James Copeland
36. Stephen Copeland
37. Henry Dillon
38. Saml. Dillon
39. Wm. Allen
40. James McBoots(?)
41. Simon Sims
42. James Bradssaw
43. Sampson Eldridge
44. John Eldridge

----- ? --- Gardenhire
W. Harrison
John Partrick
Stephen Sewel
John Grayham
Charles Staples
Greenwood Harrison
76. Andrew Swallows
77. Stephen Mayfield
78. James Mayfield
79. Jacckurst (as written)
80. Isacc Taylor
81. Richard Mullins
82. Nelson Ray
83. Henry Gillmore
84. Wm. Taylor
85. Hall Dilling
86. Emstort Walker
87. Merel Littel
88. Wm. Harlow
James ----- ?
Daniel Erwin

Next page of the original
Carter Dalton
Joseph Garrott
John Flat
Joseph Harris
David Harris
Jesse Hull
John Huddleston
Allen Brack
John Camon (or Cannon ?)
John Cargile
James Zachrey
John Grimsley
Joel Brock
Gideon Thomas
James Mabry
Daniel Camon
Isaac Shell
Wm. Gunniels (Gunneels ?)
John Erwin
Martin Grimsley
Vardiman Lee
Wm. Frat
Arthur Flowers
John Harris
John Goode
Benjamin Flowers
Benjamin Harrison
Frans/ McConnell
Arthur Mitchell
Arthur Babb
Tviy (?) Harp
Eli Harrison
Hiram Allen
Achilles Stephens

Next Page, original

James Willard
Tobt. Boyd
Abraham Goodpasture
Joseph Grammer
Sterling Collier
George More
Wm. Goleman
Madison Fisk
Solomon Eaves
Randal Murray
John Smart
James McRoberts
David Liles
James Woods
Daniel Liles
James Wood
Daniel Liles
Stephen Row
Henry Wood
Isaiah Row
Jacob Rook
John Davise
William Dobbs
George Gilpatrick
Henry Bailey
Jeremiah Holeman
William Officer
Walter Fisk
Tiry Harp
Eli Harrison
Hiram Allen
Achilles Stephens
Elijah Davis
Joel Cain
Thos. R. Harris
John Rolls
Thos. Masters
John W. Moore
John Goodpasture
John Savage
Reubin Witt
Arthur Goodpasture
John McCord
William Willard
Samuel Harris

Isam Johnson
James Murray
James McConnell
Isaac Hufiman
Jesse Masters

NOTE: The first census of Overton County which is preserved is for the year 1820. This is an excellent list to show many families who were living in Overton County as early as 1813. It also serves a second purpose: the Society of the United States Daughters of the War of 1812, credit for membership into their organization services rendered to 1815. This list therefore is sufficient to establish service. It is noted that there is believed to be some duplication of names on the list. However, in order to be certain that none was omitted, the entire list (duplicates and all) is given here. Where a question mark is used means that the script was bad and the name difficult to make out correctly. Where a line is drawn means that it was impossible to read the name. It is also to be remembered that these men were all of military age, offering their services to go against the Creek Indians. I consider it a very valuable document for many reasons. ERW

RECORD OF THE COMMISSIONS OF OFFICERS IN THE TENNESSEE MILITIA. 1807-1811

John Armstrong, Lieutenant. Commissioned May 30, 1807
Alexander Baxter, Ensign. Commissioned May 30, 1807
Benjamin Cannon, Lieutenant. Commissioned Oct. 13, 1807
John Copeland, Captain. Commissioned May 30, 1807
Richard Copeland, Junr., Lieutenant. Commissioned May,30,1807
Stephen Copeland, Lieut-Colonel. Commandant. May 30, 1807
John B. Cross, First Major. Commissioned May 30, 1807
Josiah Derham, Ensign. Commissioned May 30, 1807
James Goodpasture, Captain. Commissioned May 30, 1807
Spencer Groger, Ensign. Commissioned May 30, 1807
James Harrison, Junr., Ensign. Commissioned Oct. 13, 1807
Michael Hickey, Captain. Commissioned Oct. 13, 1807
Thomas Hill, Ensign. Commissioned Oct. 13, 1807
John Jones, Lieutenant. Commissioned May 30, 1807
William Levingston, Ensign. Commissioned May 30, 1807
Menai Martin, Lieutenant. Commissioned Oct. 13, 1807
James Mathews, Captain. Commissioned Oct. 13, 1807
Charles Matlock, Captain. Commissioned May 30, 1807
James M. Maxwell, Lieutenant. Commissioned May 30, 1807
John Morriss, Ensign. Commissioned May 30, 1807
Joseph Norman, Lieutenant. Commissioned Oct. 13, 1807

Robert Oneal, Captain. Commissioned May 30, 1807
Charles Sevier, Second Major. Commissioned May 30,1807
Jacob Swallow, Ensign. Commissioned Oct. 13, 1807
James Turner, Captain. Commissioned May 30, 1807
Peter Williams, Lieutenant. Commissioned May 30, 1807
Peter Williams, Captain. Commissioned Oct. 13, 1807
James Witt, Ensign. Commissioned Oct. 13, 1807
William Young, Captain. Commissioned May 30, 1807

Matthew Babb, Ensign 34th regiment. Sept. 28, 1808
Daniel Brown, Captain 35th regiment. Sept. 21, 1808
Daniel Brown, Captain 35th regiment. Oct. 15, 1808
William Callahan, Ensign. March 22, 1808
Thomas Dale, Lieutenant 35th regiment. Sept. 21, 1808
William Copeland, Lieutenant 35th regiment. Oct. 15, 1808
William Daniel, Lieutenant 34th regiment. Sept.28, 1808
Michael Early, Lieutenant 34th regiment. Sept. 28, 1808
John Elsey, Ensign 35th regiment. Oct. 15, 1808
William Evans, Captain. March 22, 1808
Middleton Fannon, Lieutenant 35th regiment. Sept.15,1808
James Gilliland, Ensign 35th regiment. Sept. 15, 1808
William Hudspeath, Lieutenant 35th regiment. Sept. 15, 1808
Charles Katron, Captain 34th regiment. Sept. 28, 1808
William McCord, Ensign 35th regiment. Sept. 15, 1808
Jacob Mayberry, Lieutenant. March 22, 1808
Isaac Oats, Captain. March 22, 1808
Squire Poteet, Captain 35th regiment. Sept. 15, 1808
John Rawlings, Lieutenant 35th regiment. Sept. 15, 1808
Iri Smith, Ensign. March 22, 1808
William Walker, Ensign 35th regiment. Oct. 15, 1808
Elijah Weaver, Captain 34th regiment. Sept. 28, 1808
David Williams, Captain 35th regiment. Sept. 15, 1808
John Williams, Lieutenant. March 22, 1808
Abel Willis, Captain 35th regiment. Sept. 15, 1808
Henry Willis, Ensign 34th regiment. Sept. 28, 1808
Joseph Hawkins Windell, Adjutant. March 26, 1808

John Armstrong, Lieutenant 35th regiment. April 8, 1809
Fielden Hudleston, Ensign 35th regiment. April 8, 1809

James Berry, Captain 35th regiment. November 29, 1810
Branter Clark, Lieutenant 35th regiment. November 29, 1810
George Duncan, Lieutenant 35th regiment. November 29, 1810
James Finley, Captain 35th regiment. November 29, 1810
John Garner, Ensign 35th regiment. November 29, 1810
Aaron Sharp, Ensign 35th regiment. November 29, 1810
Samuel P. Stewart, Ensign 35th regiment. November 29, 1810

Isaac Hill, Lieutenant 35th regiment. August 9, 1811
Willie Huddleston, Captain 35th regiment. Aug. 9, 1811
Thomas Kennedy, Captain 35th regiment. August 9, 1811
Andrew Means, Ensign 35th regiment. October 11, 1811
Mo. Madlock, Captain 35th regiment. October 11, 1811
Thomas Officer, Captain 35th regiment. August 9, 1811

Robert Parker, Ensign 35th regiment. August 9, 1811
Benjamin Parrott, Lieutenant 35th regiment. August 9, 1811
Thomas Sexton, Lieutenant 35th regiment. October 11, 1811
Caleb Shot, Ensign 35th regiment. August 9, 1811
David Stewart, Lieutenant 35th regiment. August 9, 1811
Samuel Tindle, Captain 35th regiment. August 9, 1811
Patterson Walker, Ensign 35th regiment. October 11, 1811
Harman Witt, Lieutenant 35th regiment. August 9, 1811

==

NOTE OF INFORMATION:

Most, practically all, the Jackson County, Tennessee records were destroyed when the Courthouse was destroyed.

Smith County, Tennessee records are excellent, except for some early marriages which are missing.

Morgan County, Tennessee records are in fair condition but do not seem to be very complete.

In 1770 the Long Hunters, 40 in number, played a very important part in the history of Cumberland County, Kentucky and that part of Tennessee which became Overton County. All of the names of the Long Hunters are not certainly known. Some of them were: James Knox, Richard Knox, Obediah Terrell, (it is said Obed's River was named for him), Uriah Stone, James Graham, John Montgomery, Abraham Bledsoe, Richard Skaggs, Henry Skaggs, William Baker and others.

John Reneau as assignee of William Reneau obtained land which was claimed to be in Cumberland Co., Ky. Aug. 29, 1798. Contained 200 acres on Wolf River below a branch called Lick Branch.

William Wood had land on east fork of Lick Branch on Obey River, 200 acres, in 1798. Isaac Denton had 200 acres on north side Wolf River, Aug. 30, 1798. These lands were supposed to be in Cumberland County, Ky., and were certainly on the State line.

Christopher Myers had 400 acres on Lick Branch of Wolf River in 1801. This land was claimed to be in Cumberland County, Kentucky at that time.

The Cumberland County, Kentucky, courthouse burned in 1933 and most of their records were destroyed, except a few which Mrs. Nora C. McGee had in her home for the purpose of transcribing. These were the marriages 1799-1882, part of which are preserved.

PENSIONERS IN OVERTON & ADJOINING COUNTIES

Early Alberton, list of 1832, age 78 years, served in North Carolina Militia. Pensioned in Overton County.

Jesse Ashlock, in the 1832 list, age 74 years. Also shown in 1840 pension census. Served in North Carolina Militia. Pensioned in Overton County, Tennessee.

Andrew Beaty, List of 1832, age 74 years. Served in the North Carolina line. Pensioned in Fentress County, Tenn.

Joseph Brooks, list of pensioned 1828. Served in the second Regiment U. S. Rifles, War of 1812. Pensioned in Overton County, Tenn.

Cornelius Carmack, in the list of 1832 and 1840. In 1832 was age 75 years. Served in the Virginia line. In 1840 lived with John Carmack in Overton County, and drew pension.

John Carswell, list of 1832, age 70 years. Served in the Virginia line. Pensioned in Overton County, Tenn.

Lucy Chapman, widow, in list of 1840, age 70 years. Pensioned in Fentress County.

Willis Coal, list of 1832, age 71 years. Served in North Carolina line. Drew pension in Fentress County, Tenn.

Richard Copeland, list of 1818, age 73 years. Served in the North Carolina Troops. Drew pension in Overton County, Tennessee.

Isaac Crabtree, list of 1832, age 76 years. Served in the Virginia line. Pensioned in Overton County, Tennessee.

Isaac Dotty (Dotey ?) list of 1818, age 84 years. Served in North Carolina Troops. Drew pension in Overton County, Tennessee.

Isaac Fancher, list of 1828. He served in the 7th Regiment of U. S. Infantry, War of 1812. Pensioned in Overton County.

John Felkins. 1818 list of pensioners, age 74 years. Served in North Carolina line. Pensioned in Overton County.

Smith Ferrell. 1832 list, age 76 years. Also in the 1840 census of pensioners. Served in North Carolina Militia. In 1832 he was granted pension and then lived in Monroe County, but in 1840 was in Overton County.

Rowland Flowers, served in the Virginia Troops. Pensioned in Fentress County, Tennessee. He is shown in the 1840 list with widow Ann Flowers, age 78, on pension. She was living with Archibald Stone in Fentress County.

Joseph French, in the list of 1832, age 74 years. Served in the Virginia Militia. Pensioned in Fentress County.

David Gentry Senr., list of 1840, age 97. Pensioned in Overton County.

Walter Greer, list of 1832, age 75 years. Served in the Virginia Militia. Pensioned in Overton County.

Charles Harman, list of 1832, age 71 years. Also in list of 1840. Served in the Virginia line. In 1832 he was in Overton County, but in 1840 he was in Jackson County, Tenn.

George Helm, list of 1818, age 83 years. Served in the Maryland line. Also shown in the 1840 list. Pensioned from Fentress County.

George Henderson, list of 1840, age 81 years. Pensioned in Overton County.

Robert Hill, list of 1818, age 85 years. Served in the Virginia Troops. Pensioned in Overton County.

Henry Hoover, list of 1832, age 79 years. Also in 1840 census of pensioned. Served in the Virginia line. In 1832 he was in Fentress County, but in 1840 he was in Overton County.

William Philips Senr., in 1840 list of pensioners, age 91 years. Overton County.

John Richardson, list 1832, age 74 years. North Carolina line. Overton County.

Thomas Scott Senr., 1832 list, age 79 years. Served in North Carolina line. Pensioned Fentress County.

Andrew Shortridge, in the 1840 list, age 85 years. Served in the Virginia Troops. Drew pension in Fentress County. His widow, Nancy Shortridge, also drew pension.

Andree Swallow, in the list of 1832, age 74 years, and also in list 1840. Pensioned in Overton County.

Ambrose Thacker, in list 1832, age 76 years. Served in the North Carolina line. Pensioned in Fentress County.

Jonathan Tipton, in list 1832, age 84 years. Served in North Carolina. Died January 18, 1833. Pensioned from Overton County.

Thomas Travis, in the list of 1832, age 75 years. Pensioned in Fentress County. He served in the Pennsylvania line.

Jesse Westmoreland, list of 1832, age 80 years. Pensioned in Fentress County.

Isaac Beaty, served in North Carolina. Pensioned 1835 in Overton County, Tennessee.

John Briggs, served in Virginia line, and was pensioned in Overton County, shown in the list of 1840

Richard Copeland, served in North Carolina. Pensioned in Overton County, in 1835.

Ben Johnson served in North Carolina. Pensioned in 1835 in

Overton County.

James Ashlock, list of 1840 in Overton County. Served in North Carolina.

Early Albertson, served in North Carolina. Pensioned in 1835 in Overton County.

Henry Hoover Senr. Pensioned in 1840 (1835) Overton County.

James Harrison. Served in Virginia. Pensioned in 1835 in Overton County.

George Henerson, in the list of 1840, aged 81 years. Pensioner of Overton County.

William Phillips Senr., in list of 1840, age 91 years. Pensioned in Overton County.

Benjamin Reeder (Reader), in list of 1840, age 80 years. Pensioned in Overton County.

Andrew Swallows served in North Carolina. He is in list of 1835 and 1840. His age in 1835 shown as 80 years. Pensioned in Overton County.

Samuel Tays in list of 1835, age 79 years. Also in list of 1840. Pensioned in Overton County.

Joseph Taylor Sr. in list of 1840. Pensioned in Overton Co.

Jonathan Tipton, Major in the North Carolina line. Pension list 1835, Overton County, Tenn.

Henry Dillon in list of 1840, age 80 years. Pensioned from Overton County.

David Collier in list of 1840, in Fentress County.

George Chilton in list of 1840, Fentress County.

Willis Cole served in North Carolina. In list of 1835, Fentress County.

John Palser Conatser. List of 1840. Served in the Indian Wars. Pensioned from Fentress County.

William Doss (Dorse). List of 1835 and 1840. In 1835 was 78 years of age. He served in the Indian Wars.

Benjamin Davis, list of 1840. Pensioned in Fentress County.

Joseph French. Served in Virginia. Pensioned and in list of Fentress County.

Timothy Gawney. Served in North Carolina. Pensioned from Fentress County.

Bailey Owens. Served in North Carolina. Pensioned in 1835, aged 82 years. Also in list of 1840. Fentress County.

Sam Riley, list of 1840 for Fentress County.

John Smith in list of 1840 from Fentress County.

George Skelton served in North Carolina. In pension list of 1835 from Fentress County.

The following pension list of 1883 shows the number of pension, the County, the postoffice, the reason for pension, and date placed on pension.

84110 John Smyers. P. O. Boles, Clay Co., Tenn. injured and left foot and both arms injured. Placed on pension August, 1867.

115110 Joseph Brummelt. P. O. Butler's Landing. Injured left hip. On Pension January 1872. Clay County, Tenn.

32162 Rachel Savage. P. O. Celina, Clay County. Widow of War of 1812. Placed on pension January 1882.

114344 James M. Tolman. P. O. Celina, Clay Co. Injury to abdomen by fall. Placed on pension November 1871.

115940 Wm. A. Overstreet. P. O. Celina, Clay County. Chronic rheumatism. Pensioned March 1872.

12648 Nancy Burrus. Celina, Clay County. Placed on pension December 1878.

165278 Wm. H. Morrow. P. O. Celina, Clay County. Injury in left leg. Pensioned March 1880.

213668 James Racener. P. O. Clementsville, Clay Co. Injury in right leg. Pensioned 1882.

138659 Shelton Craighead. P. O. Clementsville, Clay County. Chronic rheumatism. Pensioned April 1876.

211488 Stewart H. Vinson. P. O. Clementsville, Clay County. Disease of the eye. Pensioned June 1882.

150303 Mary York, P. O. Clementsville, Clay County, mother and dependent of soldier. Pensioned May 1871.

207980 Jonathan S. Harlan. P. O. Clementsville, Clay County. Chronic Diarrah. Pensioned May 1882.

32455 Rutha Plumlee. P. O. Clementsville, Clay County, widow of soldier of War 1812. Pensioned June 1882.

18156 Rosanna Hale, P. O. Willow Grove, Clay County. Pensioned Feby. 1879.

8738 Elias Bowden P. O. Boatland, Fentress County, Survivor of the war of 1812. Pensioned November 1871.

93869 Hillery Sells, P. O. Jamestown, Fentress County. wounded in the hip. Pensioned November 1868.

163161 Wm. Brannon, P. O. Jamestown, Fentress County, frost bitten right foot. Pensioned October 1879.

83998 Souverina Guffey, P. O. Jamestown, Fentress County, widow of a soldier. Pensioned May 1871.

118332 Emeline Carney, P. O. Jamestown, Fentress County, widow of soldier. Pensioned Sept. 1868.

137247 Malinda Choate, P. O. Jamestown, Fentress County, widow of soldier. Pensioned December 1869.

185364 William J. Carney, P. O. Jamestown, Fentress County, minor heir of a soldier. Pensioned August 1879.

93728 Martha Wirmington, P. O. Jamestown, Fentress County, widow of a soldier. Pensioned May 1867.

185077 Wm. W. Wood, P. O. Jamestown, Fentress County, Minor of a soldier. Pensioned September 1881.

92350 Anna Storie, P. O. Jamestown, Fentress County, Widow of a soldier. Pensioned March 1874.

158294 Eliza Ann Turner, P. O. Jamestown, Fentress County, widow, Pensioned June 1872.

133413 Mary Ann Hale, P. O. Jamestown, Fentress County, widow, Pensioned August 1869.

119093 Mary Ann Hoover, P. O. Jamestown, Fentress County. widow, Pensioned Sept. 1869.

52044 Henry P. Hould, P. O. Jamestown, Fentress County, injury in thigh, Pensioned November 1865.

121161 Simeon Hindes, P. O. Jamestown, Fentress County, contracted consumption in service. Pensioned January 1873.

9644 Polly Oxford, P. O. Jamestown, Fentress County, widow of soldier of 1812. On pension October 1878.

115763 Mary Mullins, P. O. Jamestown, Fentress County, widow of soldier. Pensioned July 1868.

112224 Eliza E. Lankford, P. O. Jamestown, Fentress County, widow of soldier. Pensioned April 1868.

101053 Deborah Evans, P. O. Jamestown, Fentress County, widow, Pensioned Sept. 1867

149021 Sarah A. Edwards, P. O. Jamestown, Fentress County, widow, Pensioned March 1871.

121641 Susan Beaty, P. O. Jamestown, Fentress County, dependent mother, Pensioned Nov. 1868.

140193 Eliza King, P. O. Jamestown, Fentress County, dependent mother, Pensioned Feb. 1870.

159451 Hannah Davidson, P. O. Jamestown, Fentress County, widow, Pensioned August 1872.

51095 And. J. Northrup, P. O. Jamestown, Fentress County, injury to left hand. Pensioned November 1865.

214024 Wm. Petty P. O. Pall Mall, Fentress County, injury to breast, Pensioned June 1882.

178540 Lucretia Dunkin P. O. Pall Mall, Fentress County, dependent mother, Pensioned Sept. 1877.

170398 Jane Crabtree, P. O. Pall Mall, Fentress County, dependent mother, Pensioned July 1875.

189642 Mary Wright, P. O. Pall Mall. dependent mother. Pensioned Sept. 1880.

184858 Nancy Reagan, P. O. Pall Mall, Fentress County, dependent mother, Pensioned July 1879.

191765 Lucinda Hider, P. O. Pall Mall, Fentress County, Dependent mother, Pensioned April 1881.

132935 Mitchell R. Millsaps, P. O. Pall Mall, Fentress County chronic rheumatism. Pensioned April 1875.

29670 Nellie Looper, P. O. Pall Mall, Fentress County. Widow of War of 1812. Pensioned June 1880.

27001 Vinia Pults, P. O. Pall Mall, Fentress County. Widow War 1812. Pensioned Sept. 1879.

26488 Isabell Smith, P. O. Pall Mall, Fentress County. widow of War of 1812. Pensioned August 1879.

31269 Clara Flowers, P. O. Pall Mall, Fentress County, widow of War 1812. Pensioned March 1881.

10003 Louisa Froggs, P. O. Pall Mall, Fentress County, widow of War of 1812. Pensioned Oct. 1878.

14967 Elizabeth Wright, P. O. Pall Mall, Fentress County, widow of War 1812. Pensioned Jan. 1879.

172804 Myria Honeycutt, P. O. Beaver Hill, Overton County, widow, Pensioned March 1876.

172719 Wm. P. McKnight, P. O. Livingston, Overton County, child of a soldier. Pensioned -------

31747 Patsey Harris, P. O. Livingston, Overton County, widow of soldier of War of 1812, Pensioned May 1881.

30834 Margaret Tays, P. O. Livingston, Overton County, widow of soldier of the War of 1812. Pensioned Nov. 1880.

16106 Mary Reed, P. O. Livingston, Overton County, widow of War 1812. Pensioned January 1879.

6615 Patsey Mullins, P. O. Livingston, Overton County, widow of War of 1812. Pensioned June 1875.

20562 Alfred Harris, P. O. Livingston, Overton County, Survivor of War 1812. Pensioned April 1873.

9122 Hiram M. Allen, P. O. Livingston, Overton County, Survivor of War 1812. Pensioned December 1871.

8954 Jno. W. Hall, P. O. Livingston, Overton County, had chronic Diarrah. Pensioned.

154249 Harriet Taylor, P. O. Livingston, Overton County, widow, Pensioned Nov. 1871.

121777 Louisa Coalman, P. O. Livingston, Overton County, widow. Pensioned December 1868.

183359 Moses Ferren, P. O. Livingston, Overton County, injured in abdomen. Pensioned Feb. 1881.

136325 Perlina Goolsby, P. O. Livingston, Overton County, widow, Pensioned Nov. 1869.

32592 Harriette Knox, P. O. Livingston, Overton County, widow of War 1812. Pensioned August 1882.

6376-? Charlotte Smith, P. O. Monroe, Overton County, widow. Pensioned February 1868.

114850 Caroline Hull, P. O. Monroe, Overton County, widow. Pensioned November 1868.

137400 May J. Hull, P. O. Monroe, Overton County, widow. Pensioned December 1869.

110520 George W. Garrett, P. O. Monroe, Overton County. Contracted Chronic Diarrah. Pensioned October 1869.

513 Winner Lynn, P. O. Monroe, Overton County, widow. Pensioned January 1869.

86442 James Tranbarger, P. O. Monroe, Overton County. Was wounded in the left hand. Pensioned May 1871.

64798 Margaret Surber, P. O. Monroe, Overton County, widow. Pensioned March 1872.

138198 Jesse Pearson Crouch, P. O. Monroe, Overton County. Wounded in the right forearm. Pensioned March 1876.

84287 Rebecca Ragin, P. O. Nettle Carrier, Overton County, widow. Pensioned September 1867.

151205 Mary Robbins, P. O. Nettle Carrier, Overton County, widow. Pensioned June 1871.

5817 Sarah Douglass, P. O. Oak Hill, Overton County, widow of War of 1812. Pensioned December 1873.

29691 Blessed Braington, P. O. Oakley, Overton County. Survivor of the War of 1812. Pensioned June 1880.

114033 Robert F. Boles, P. O. Poteet, Overton County. Was injured in the right knee during service. Pensioned October, 1871.

216436 Wm. Bowman, P. O. Qualls, Overton County. He was injured in the spine and abdomen. Pensioned August, 1882.

119441 Thomas J. Reagon, P. O. Qualls, Overton County. He was wounded in the right leg in service. Pensioned Oct.1872.

67436 Mary Turner, P. O. West Fork, Overton County, widow. Pensioned June 1867.

59362 Margaret C. Bicknell, P. O. West Fork, Overton County. Widow. Pensioned March 1868.

74883 Robins Tennessee (or Tennessee Robins ?) P. O. West Fork, Overton County. widow. Pensioned June 1867.

153911 Charlotte Sells, P. O. West Fork, Overton County. Widow. Pensioned February 1872.

145026 Mary Smith, P. O. West Fork, Overton County. widow. Pensioned September 1870.

122397 Louisa Sells, P. O. West Fork, Overton County. widow. Pensioned December 1868.

183490 Eliza A. Cowan, P. O. Chanute, Pickett County, widow of soldier. There was also a minor child who received pension. Pensioned March 1879.

113853 Jacob H. Sells, P. O. Olympus, Pickett County. He contracted a disease of the kidneys in service. Pensioned September 1871.

110806 James D. Reagan, P. O. Olympus, Pickett County. A condition of the left hip contracted in service. Pensioned May 1871.

96888 Wm. Mullin, P. O. Olympus, Pickett County. Wound in left leg. Pensioned April 1869.

116383 Mary Garrett, P. O. Olympus, Pickett County. Was mother (dependent) of a soldier. Pensioned December, 1868.

73768 Mary Garrett, P. O. Olympus, Pickett County. Widow of soldier. Pensioned November 1867.

83537 Abigail Conatser, P. O. Olympus, Pickett County. widow. Pensioned January 1870.

173467 Charles M. Clark, P. O. Olympus, Pickett County. Minor child of a soldier. Pensioned May 1876.

49666 Temperance Wilson, P. O. Olympus, Pickett County. widow. Pensioned September 1867.

11428 Abraham Jones, P. O. Olympus, Pickett County. Survivor of the War of 1812. Pensioned January 1872.

116384 Mary Beaty, P. O. Olympus, Pickett County. Dependent mother of soldier. Pensioned December 1868.

159698 Henry A. Clark, P. O. Olympus, Pickett County. Contracted consumption. Pensioned May 1879.

121587 William R. --- ? ---, P. O. Travisville. Wounded in right arm. Pensioned February 1873.

103035 Matilda J. Sells, P. O. Travisville, Pickett County. widow. Pensioned November 1867.

216257 Daniel Malone, P. O. Travisville, Pickett County. Disease in the left leg. Pensioned August 1882.

52606 Nancy Lawson, P. O. Travisville, Pickett County. widow. Pensioned August 1865.

121906 Zilpha Beaty, P. O. Travisville, Pickett County, widow. Pensioned December 1868.

116024 Nancy Cooper, P. O. Travisville, Pickett County. widow. Pensioned July 1871.

135966 Delia Perdue, P. O. Travisville, Pickett County. Mother of soldier. Pensioned November 1869.

61630 James P. West, P. O. Travisville, Pickett County. Wounded in right thigh. Pensioned April 1866.

NOTE: The list for Putman County is being included here as some of those in Putman County were of families who settled early in Overton County.

30163 Hannah Carr, P. O. Bloomington, Putman County. Widow of War of 1812. Pensioned August, 1880.

164764 Meredith Gentry, P. O. Bloomington, Putman County. Had rheumatism. Pensioned February 1880.

3478 Ann Doughty, P. O. Bloomington, Putman County. Widow of soldier of the War of 1812. Pensioned August 1872.

82884 Adoniran J. Way, P. O. Byrne, Putman County. Wounded in the neck and shoulder. Pensioned July 1867.

23263 America Barks, P. O. Byrne, Putman County. Widow of 1812 soldier. Pensioned April 1879.

19352 Elizabeth Montgomery, P. O. Byrne, Putman County. widow of War of 1812. Pensioned March 1879.

188942 Martha Lewis, P. O. Byrne, Putman County. widow. Pensioned June 1880.

158459 Sarah Erwin, (alias). P. O. Byrne, Putman County. Widow. Pensioned June 1872. Name also given Irwin.

179792 Elenor Bruce, P. O. Byrne, Putman County. Mother of soldier. Pensioned January 1878.

199931 Wm. J. Keylon, P. O. Calf Killer, Putman County. Contracted disease of the lungs in service. Pensioned December 1881.

5700 Elizabeth Byers, P. O. Cookeville, Putman County. Widow of the War of 1812. Pensioned October 1873.

1936 Sarah Bohaman, P. O. Cookeville, Putman County. Widow of the war of 1812. Pensioned 1872, in March.

14355 James Peek, P. O. Cookeville, Putman County. Survivor of the War of 1812. Pensioned March 1872.

89624 Andrew F. Byers, P. O. Cookeville, Putman County. Lost right leg in service. Pensioned --------- .

129754 Arminda Smith, P. O. Cookeville, Putman County, widow. Pensioned May 1869.

162583 Carter Harris, P. O. Cookeville, Putman County. Contracted disease of the eyes. Pensioned October 1879.

140519 Wm. S. Gilliem. P. O. Cookeville, Putman County. Disease in the eyes. Pensioned August 1876.

12217 Samuel Miller, P. O. Cookeville, Putman County. Survivor of the War of 1812. Pensioned February 1872.

30112 Elenor Perkins, P. O. Cookeville, Putman County. Widow of the War of 1812. Pensioned August 1880.

182369 David Norris, P. O. Cookeville, Putman County.Father (dependent) of a deceased soldier. Pensioned November 1878.

117932 Caroline Barr, P. O. Cookeville, Putman County. widow. Pensioned August 1868.

27085 Elizabeth Terry, P. O. Cookeville, Putman County. Widow of War of 1812. Pensioned September 1879.

32809 Elizabeth Terry, P. O. Cookeville, Putman County. Widow of the War of 1812. Pensioned December 1882.

4237 Susannah Davis, P. O. Cookeville, Putman County, widow of the War of 1812. Pensioned November 1872.

128400 Elizabeth Vickers, P. O. Cookeville, Putman County, widow. Pensioned April 1869.

155583 Joseph Kinner, P. O. Cookeville, Putman County. Wounded in the left hip. Pensioned September 1878.

6192 Elizabeth Boyd, P. O. Pekin, Putman County. Widow of War of 1812. Pensioned June 1874.

161420 Michael Campbell, P. O. Pekin, Putman County. widow. Pensioned March 1873.

162320 Matilda W. Bush, P. O. Pekin, Putman County. widow. Pensioned May 1873.

127895 Hiser V. Richardson, P. O. Pine Fork, Putman County. Wounded in right leg in service. Pensioned April 1874.

113150 Joseph C. Kerr, P. O. Silver Point. Wounded in right foot. Pensioned Aug. 1871.

115354 Wm. G. Davis P. O. Window Cliff, Putman County. Fractured left leg in service. Pensioned Jan. 1872.

==

MISC. NOTES -------- OVERTON COUNTY, TENNESSEE

Adward N. Cullom lived in the 11th District of Overton County in 1850. He was then 56 years of age, and was born in Kentucky. His wife was Hannah (or Nannah) born also in Kentucky, age 50 years in 1850. They had a very large family, consisting of Alvan age 24, Lucinda age 22, James C. age 20 (a merchant at the time), Susan age 18, William age 16, Edward age 13, Henry C. age 12, Daniel W. age 12, Thomas J. age 9, Richard L. age 7, Permelia F. age 4, Butt age 2 and possibly younger children born after 1850. All the children were born in Tennessee.

William Elder was living in the 11th District of Overton County in 1850. He was then age 66 years and was born in North Carolina. His wife was named Patsey and was then 65 years of age, also born in North Carolina. They had a family of children in 1850.

Landon Armstrong was born in North Carolina. In 1850 he gave his age as 58 years, and his wife Ann gave her age as 58 years stating that she was born in Kentucky. They were residing in the 11th District of Overton County, Tennessee in 1850 with a family.

Elizabeth Martin was evidently a widow living in Overton County in 1850, at which time she was about 63 years of age, and was born in North Carolina. In her household in 1850 lived William Martin age 25, Lucinda Martin age 41, Nancy Martin age 34, Elizabeth Martin age 28, and Menan Martin age 20, all born in Tennessee.

The Organ family came to Overton County from Virginia. Christopher Organ, age 46, was born in Virginia. He was an L. P. Preacher. In 1850 in his household were: Matilda age 29, Frances age 4, Donnel age 1 and Mary age 1, all born in Tennessee.

John L. Brady, a native of North Carolina, age 66 years in 1850 was living in Overton County. His wife was May, and gave her age about 51 years in 1850, born in North Carolina. They had a family.

Faiden Dick or Deck, a native of North Carolina, age 78 in 1850, with wife Mary same age and native also of North Carolina, was living in the Sixth District of Overton County in 1850.

In the Seventh District of Overton County, in 1850, lived David Garroett, age 52, born in Virginia. He had a family.

Abraham Garrott, age 50, born in Virginia, also resided in Overton County in 1850. His wife was Eliza J. age

58, born in Tennessee. In 1850 they had seven children living with them. There may have been other children.

Eliza Garret, age 73, born in Virginia and who very likely was a widow, lived in Overton County in 1850, and with her was a Mary Garrett, age 71, also born in Virginia. In the same house was a considerable family in 1850. Next door lived Stephen Garrett age 48 born in Virginia, with wife Sarah, age 35, born in Tennessee and who also had a family in his household.

Thomas Cope came from North Carolina to Overton County. In 1850 he gave his age as 75 years. He had a family.

John Huddleston, a native of Virginia, gave his age as 66 years in 1850. In his household at that time lived Ann Huddleston, age 74, born in Virginia. Joel G. age 31, James age 18, William age 16 and Sarah A. age 14, all born in Tennessee.

Thomas Flowers and his wife, Nancy, were living in the County of Overton in the 11th District in 1850. He gave his age as 65 and she 61, both born in Virginia.

Henry Henson, age about 81, a native of Virginia, with wife Elizabeth, age about 79, born in North Carolina, and a considerable family were living in Overton County in 1850.

Sloan Cullom was a lawyer living in Overton County in 1850. His age at that time was about 53 years. He was a native of Kentucky. His wife was named Susan, and at that time her age was about 50 years, also a native of Kentucky. They had a family.

Joseph Garrett, Senr., was living in the Tenth District of Overton County in 1850. He was a native of Virginia, age about 67 years. In his household: Juda age 62, born Va., Josiah age 20, John age 13, Jasper age 7, Juda age 6, all born in Tennessee. Nearby lived Shadric Garret age 42, born in Virginia, with a family consisting of Catharine age 24, Eliza age 7, Mary age 6, Malina age 4, all born in Tennessee.

George Christian, age about 81, and Elizabeth, age about 66, born in Virginia, with a family resided in Overton County in 1850.

The Looper family of Overton County came from North Carolina.

Benjamin Norred came from South Carolina to Overton County and had a family. He was born about 1781 or 1782.

Archibald Story age 68 a native of Virginia, a stone cutter, settled in Overton County before 1850. In his family were Elizabeth age 65 born Virginia, and Elizabeth age 27, Mary age 25, Archibald age 21, and Nancy age 16, all born in Tennessee.

Anthony and Catherine Flowers, natives of Virginia, age 75 and 77 years, came to Overton County, and established a home and reared a considerable family.

Sianah Pariss, age 70, a native of Virginia, was living in Overton County 1850. She was evidently a widow at that time, with a family living with her. She lived in the 12th District of the county. Nearby lived a Willis Pariss with a family who was possibly a son of Sianah, and not far away was Sicily Parriss, possibly also of the same family.

The Richardsons of Overton County were mostly natives of Virginia, but some of them were born in Kentucky, indicating that they migrated through Kentucky into Overton County. This family is well represented in Overton, Pickett, Clay and Fentress to this day.

Henry Sells was a native of Pennsylvania. He was residing in the 7th Civil District of Overton County in 1850. With him was Margaret age 55, born in Tennessee. Next door lived David Sells age 52 born in Tennessee, with a family.

The Mainards came from North Carolina, while the Mullins came from Virginia. The Martins came from North Carolina. Some of the Martins may have come from Virginia. The Willis family came into Overton County through Kentucky. The Edens were South Carolina stock, migrating first to Kentucky then to Overton County. Elias Edens in the census of 1850 shows his age as 68 years, a native of South Carolina. Sarah his wife was age 65, also born South Carolina, while their children were mostly born in Kentucky; namely, William, Henry, Elias and A. K.

There seems to have been Garrotts and Garretts, possibly two distinct families, who settled in Overton County. These are not to be confused; however, careful research -- not having been made at this time -- may show them one and the same originally.

Arthur Goodpasture age 68 a native of Virginia, with wife Jane age 62 born South Carolina, lived in the Third District of the county in 1850. The Goodpasture family had long been prominent in this county and the adjoining counties.

The Dentons trace their lineage to Virginia, back into New Jersey, New York and to the New England states to Richard Denton, one of the earliest ministers in America.

INDEX TO WILL BOOK 1870-1891, OVERTON COUNTY.

==

Will of W. W. Chilton, dated June 7, 1881. Names wife Eliza. Children. Mahala Stinson's children, namely - Joshua, John, Aaron B., James William and Melina Stinson; Elizabeth Dewberry; Joshua Chilton; Lafeyette Chilton; John Chilton; and A. P. Chilton.

Will of Delila Looper. My companion Magnes Looper decd. Son A. C. Looper. Son Magnes Looper. Daughter Nelly Speck. Son Joseph Looper, Son Lewis Looper, Daughter Mahala Looper. Daughter Matilda Speck. Daughter Delila Looper. Executor A. C. Looper. Dated June 29, 1866.

==

SUPREME COURT TRANSCRIPTS

Original papers on file Tennessee State Archives, Nashville, Tennessee.

Obediah Bradshaw & others VS William Beach and Others. 1823.

Overton County, Tennessee, Third Judicial Circuit Court. John Thurman, Solomon Silcon (?), Simon Huddleston, Benjamin Poore, John Ric--- ?, Joshua Storie and Catherine Storie his wife and etc.
(Abstract of file). Mentions a mill on Wolf River. Reference is made to Billy Beach. Refers to certain negroes -- Tom, Fanny, Solomon and others. Refers to Joseph Evans. One paper refers to going to North Carolina on business. Another paper mentions Lewis Carlton in North Carolina. One paper says that the family of William Beach consisted of six or seven children. There is mention of a place called Barksville, thirty-three miles from ------- (torn).

Joshua Storie, Sr., on oath states he was acquinted with Mr. Bradshaw before coming from North Carolina and that he lived in the same house with me two or three weeks, then I moved away and never seen him for about thirteen years, when I saw him at my son Joshua Stories, he did not know me. When I started away my son told him who I was and he caught me in his arms. Signed Joshua Storie. Witnessed by Jas. Whiteside, J. P.

Catharine Storie being sworn, age 44 years, says she had a long acquaintance with Mr. Bradshaw and his wife, as well as Beach. She knew them twelve or thirteen years in North Carolina. She understood that Mr. Bradshaw when on his death bed was 80 years of age. "Out conversation was twelve or thirteen years ago. There was mention that Mr. Bradshaw had a will. Billy Beach had the negroes. Bradshaw probably conveyed property to Wm. Beach and Mrs. Bradshaw threatened to leave Mr. Bradshaw and that she would and could not live apart from her daughter at the time they were about moving to the farm bought from Mr. Storie.

Mrs. Bradshaw said that she had but one child and she would not be parted by no man on earth from her. Mrs. Bradshaw said she had never been married before she married Mr. Bradshaw. Old Mr. Bradshaw said he had to pay tax both in Tennessee and North Carolina and that he was so hard of hearing he did not want to pay tax and he always put the money in hands of Billy Beach for him to settle it. About eleven or twelve years ago the old gentleman said that Billy had been down several times after his money and he did not know what Billy done with it. Must spent it for Rum along with Abernathy's boys. He may have give it to his brother or drank it up. Said William Beach has lived with and supported Bradshaw's wife. Mr. Bradshaw said Billy Beach lived on his place.

Mrs. Bradshaw said she had given William Beach's

children some clothing both boys and girls for twenty years and some she intended for her daughter Mrs. Beach.

Another time at Mr. Brambletts, Mrs. Bradshaw was getting something in the store and said it was stuff to make bonnetts for one of the girls and intended to get each of the girls a white dress. She said most of the money Beach paid was her money. She talked about money Beach owed old Mr. Storie. Signed Catherine Storie. J. Whiteside J.P. Sworn to in Overton County, 4 June 1819.

Deposition of Joseph Evans in Overton County, 15 Feby,1820. Joseph Evans age 35 years, deposeth ----- Was present at signing of bill of sale between William Bradshaw and William Beach. Word came by boys "that lived with me" to come down there. "I" went down to Beaches and saw John Thurman in the mill yard. He said "we" go up to the old house, after going up near the barn or house in the field he turned around to me and said ---- "about to give bill of sale for three negroes from Bradshaw to Beach" Went to the house and stayed some time before Beach came there. Beach had the papers. "I cannot read so I handed it to William Beach and he read it." When it was read Mr. Bradshaw (hard of hearing) said "What is this 420 pounds put in for I never received anything." Mr. Thurman spoke up "Something put in to make it good." The old man sat and said nothing. William Beach spoke "Grandfather is you arn't willing don't do it." The old lady spoke "We are willing arn't we honey." Then Mr. Bradshaw said "I reckon so."

The negroes were called and delivered. "I was well acquainted with Mr. Bradshaw." "He was nearly deaf and blind." William Beach had lived at Hind's plantation. Bradshaw and Beach lived on the same plantation and on the place where also Mr. Dalton now lives and they moved on Thurman's place with exception of Mr. Beach living a while at Hind's plantation. Signed Jos. Evans.

Simon Huddleston deposition. Age 57 years. Had an acquaintance with Mr. Bradshaw a short time when he first came to this country. I thought his mental condition was impaired. It was by age. Mrs. Bradshaw and Beach were always present at transactions of the old man. Bradshaw lived on Wolf on Thurman place. Wm. Beach lived on the same plantation. None of Bradshaw's children lived with him at that time. Mr. Bradshaw said Beach was his grandson. Signed Simon Huddleston, Sworn Feb.15, 1820 Overton County, Tenn. William Atkinson J. P.

Deposition of Joseph McFarland taken in Sevier County, Tennessee at the house of Samuel Henry 14 May 1821. Joseph McFarland, age 44 years. He mentions being witness with Benjamin Poore to Bill of Sale. William Bradshaw to Wm. Beach for negroes. Also mentions land in North Carolina. Thurman lived in Kentucky. "I went home and told my wife what had happened. I said I was sorry I was there." Thurman proved the bill of sale in Overton County. Signed Joseph McFarland. 14 May 1821 Samuel Henry J. P.

Deposition of Levy Hinds 1818 in Overton County and also of Nancy Hinds at house of William Evans in said county 17 Feby. 1820. Levy Hinds age 45 years saith. "Acquainted with Bradshaw and Beach about five years. I lived between a half mile and three quarters. Beach had three or four head of horses. I think some cattle. Mr. Bradshaw had two waggons, three or four horses and cattle. Beach never lived with or took care of Mr. Bradshaw that I knew of. John Thurman bought Bradshaw's waggon in his lifetime. Bradshaw or Beach owned no land that I know of." "Old Mr. Bradshaw supported the negroes. I understand they came to this county together and lived near each other until Mr. Bradshaw died and they lived on Thurman place when he died but they farmed separately. None of Bradshaw's children lived with him since my acquaintance." Signed Levy Hinds.

Nancy Hinds age 34 years deposeth -- "Mr. Beach moved across the river on McIver land. Thurman offered to build a house for Mr. Beach on the opposite side of the river and and was afraid Mr. Thurman would not do it and they were sure of the place they had and she intended to stay on it. I lived about one half mile from them three or four years while he lived on Thurman place and there died. Said Bradshaw made a will in North Carolina -- not to her mind -- He said he would never make another." "Mrs. Bradshaw acted as a midwife I expect that she was the only one in this country. Signed Nancy (X) Hinds.

John R. Farmer, J. P. of White County. Samuel Renno sayeth - "William Beach and myself were in conversation going to Monroe. The old man was sick at the time of transaction. I knew Beach for several years. Beach and the old woman told Mr. Bradshaw that Seth Bradshaw was coming to take the negroes off." Mentions Helms and West and their wives. "Been acquainted with Joseph Evans twenty years." Signed Saml. Reno.

Overton County, deposition of Samuel Renno and Ann Renno, at house of Williams in Overton County, 16 Feby. 1820. Samuel Renno age 47 years. Lived three or four miles from Wm. Beach. Generally get grinding at his mill. Signed by Samuel Reno.

Ann Renno age 22 years. "I was living at Polly Taylors" Mentions William Johnston. "I said Grandfather what did Billy Beach give you for all your negroes" "Billy Beach never gave me anything." "I heard her tell my mother if it were not for her poor old father that he would of starved to death for he was too lazy to work for her for he done nothing but run about after one develment or another." etc. "I am the daughter of John West." Signed Ann (X) Renno.

Deposition in Overton County. Matthew Young. John Honeycutt. Mary Honeycutt. Catarine Story. May 10, 1820. Matthew Young age 36 years deposes. "Acquainted with Mr. Bradshaw at place where he died on Thurman's plantation on Wolf River about two years (in 15 and 16)" "Mr. Bradshaw told me that he was 88 the spring I moved here and then going on 89. Mr. Bradshaw said he had done a great deal for

Wm. Beach and he had not made use of it. John West was one of the old man's sons-in-law and wife. None of Mr. Bradshaw's children lived with them or in this county. Signed Matthew Young.

John Honeycutt, age 29 years, deposeth "Was acquainted with Mr. Bradshaw and Beach ten or twelve years. Mr. Bradshaw purchased a waggon from William Dooling and another from a man named Hull. No family of Bradshaw I knew but him and wife. I knew them both in North Carolina and in this state. None of Bradshaw's children lived near him only one of his sons-in-law and daughter lived on same plantation one year or thereabout." Signed John (X) Honeycutt.

Mary Honeycutt age 43 years deposeth. "Was acquainted with Mr. Bradshaw and Beach thirteen or fourteen years." Signed Mary (X) Honeycutt.

Catharine Story, age 46 years, deposition. "She was with Mr. Bradshaw in his last sickness five or six times 15th or 16th of April. two or three times. Signed Catharine (X) Story.

Overton County, Nov. 1, 1821. Depositions of John Westmoreland Junr. age 28, Samuel Reno age 48. John Williams age 33 years, William Evans age 46 years, Zachariah Enaes age 52 years.

Samuel Reno said he was at Mr. Bradshaw's when he purchased a piece of land from John McIver. It was witnessed by Mr. Bradshaw. Mr. Williams mentions John Denton and Obadiah Bradshaw in a suit pending. Signed John Williams. William Evans, deposeth, and Zachariah Ennes, deposeth that he was first acquainted with William Bradshaw in Loncoln County North Carolina. He owned valuable land negroes and other property. Mr. Bradshaw moved to Birk County (Burk) in the settlement where I lived and lived sometime. His first wife died on same plantation where he lived in Birk County. I was acquainted with Elizabeth Harper before she married Wm. Bradshaw . She was a neighbor. She was a single woman living at her father's house and was poor people, but had a little property, and my acquaintance still continued until she inter-married with Wm. Bradshaw. I never knew her to be married before. Elizabeth Harper had one child before she married Mr. Bradshaw. I was acquainted with William Beach in Birk County, while he was a single man and when Beach first lived with his grandfather Bradshaw. My knowledge Bradshaw supported Beach. There was a great difference in their age. of Bradshaw and his wife. She had great influence over him; had known him twenty five or thirty years. Beach was between eighteen and twenty then. "I am a son-in-law to one of the plaintiffs. I heard Bradshaw give his land in Lincoln County North Carolina to two of his children. He gave a negro boy to Seth Bradshaw. He gave a girl to William Bradshaw. He gave a negro child to Field Bradshaw, a son-in-law. He sold after he married the second wife, a farm."

Deposition of Joseph Evans 11 Dec. 1821 at house of Parker Young, Overton County, 11 December 1821. Age 36 years. He explains regarding a note left at house of Lewis Carlton in Town of Morgantown Burk County, North Carolina. William Beach's wife told me he was at Mr. Carter Dalton's three miles.

State of North Carolina Burke County, deposition of William W. Erwin, Esqr. in town of Morgantown, 4 May 1821. Stated. "Acquainted with William Bradshaw the elder, now deceased. Said Wm. Bradshaw was married by this deponent to Miss Elizabeth Harper a maiden lady and sister of John Harper, that pervious to her marriage with Wm. Bradshaw she had a daughter, which delieve named Prudence Harper, said Prudence married Wm. Beach the reputed grandson of Wm. Bradshaw the elder. Said Wm. Beach and wife lived in the yard and on the plantation of Wm. Bradshaw the elder and acted as overseer or manager of said Wm. Bradshaw. The deponent sold to William Beach or Wm. Bradshaw 100 acres land adjoining Wm. Bradshaw's plantation and said deposent made title to Wm. Beach and Wm. Bradshaw paid said deponent for said land, the said Wm. Beach being unable to pay for it.

William Beach continued to live with said Bradshaw for several years and said deponent was in the house several times and always supposed Wm. Beach was dependent on his grandfather William Bradshaw for his subsistance. William Bradshaw the elder was a man of considerable property, land, slaves, cattle, horses, hogs. His wife, Mrs. Bradshaw appeared to have considerable influence over him (her husband Wm. Bradshaw) and this deponent believes she intended to vest the property of William Bradshaw her husband in to hands of her daughter and son-in-law Wm. Beach. William Bradshaw the elder applied to him to prevent it. He believes this application made by the sons who lived in the neighborhood of William Bradshaw residence. Sometime before William Bradshaw removed from Burk to Lincoln. The opinion in the neighborhood that William Bradshaw was induced to move from Burke to Lincoln that his wife and her son-in-law Wm. Beach might more easily manage Wm. Bradshaw in obtaining transfer of property of said William Bradshaw old and infirm age between 80 and 90. Wm. Beach is a bad character. Signed Wm. W. Erwin. Sworn before James Avery. J. P.

Deposition of Robert Grarty (Grasty ?). He stated that he knew Bradshaw and Beach, also Mrs. Bradshaw. William Beach is a grandson of William Bradshaw the elder. Had none or little property and lived with his grandfather Wm. Bradshaw while in Burke. William Bradshaw the elder moved to Lincoln County. There is mention of Josiah Bradshaw as a son of William. Discovered Mrs. Bradshaw, wife of said William, endeavored to prevent her husband from having any conversation with his son Josiah Bradshaw. Previous to said William Bradshaw moving to Lincoln, William happened at his son Josiah's house where deponent heard Josiah ask his father why he did not rent him and go among his children like he formerly did. The old man said he disliked to have disturbance and if he went among his children as formaly and appeared friendly to them he would have constant quarrelling in his own house and get no peace. Josiah told his father "no woman should have influence over him as he supposed his wife to influence and govern him. Signed Robert (X) Grasty --- 4 May 1821.

Burke County, N. C. deposition of Elijah Largent, age 45 years and Isaac Beach about 33 years of age.

Elijah Largent deposition at courthouse in Burke County, 5 May 1821. Stated that he was acquainted with Wm. Bradshaw and his second wife, whose maiden name was Elizabeth Harper and was acquainted from defendants earliest infancy until about three years ago and she was a woman of infamous character and had a Bastard or Base born child. She had little or no property before her marriage. Knew William Bradshaw from marriage to Elizabeth Harper who was at that time about 70 years old. She knew him eight or ten years before Wm. Bradshaw left the country. She knew William Beach the grandson married Wm. Bradshaw etc. William Beach married the daughter of Mrs. Bradshaw, wife of William Bradshaw the elder. William Beach was entirely destitute oof property and depended on his grandfather for support of himself and family. William Beach married Mrs. Bradshaw's daughter Prudence Harper. Mrs. Bradshaw asked deponent if she could hold all property of William Bradshaw from his heirs and he told her that she could not. Soon after William Bradshaw sold a large portion of his negroes and moved out of Burke into Lincoln County where he lived for several years.

After which he moved to Wilkes County and this deponent was at the house of said William Bradshaw while he lived in Wilkes County, at which place Mrs. Bradshaw informed this deponent that there was a Bill of sale or deed of gift of all negroes which said Wm. Bradshaw possessed made by her husband to William Beach, and asked numerous questions about if William Beach could hold them or not. Said William Bradshaw moved to Tennessee and deponent hearing of his death obtained from Josiah Bradshaw son of William a power of attorney and a verbal permission to Tennessee to make demand of five shears of said negroes to said Wm. Beach, who was them Administrator and he claimed as his own the property. William Beach was totally destitute of the truth.

Deposition of Isaac Beach, a brother of William Beach and William at times had cattle, etc. and he also knew William Bradshaw the elder. Signed Isaac (x) Beach.

North Carolina Wilkes County, Wm. Lenorr a J. P. 30 April 1821. Depositions of Lewis Carlton, Elizabeth Carlton, Benjamin Beach, George Helm agent for complainant.

Lewis Carlton, Stated he knew William Bradshaw twelve or fifteen years ago. He purchased a tract of land from Joshua Story adjoining his own land and settled there. They became friends. He was there three or four years. William Beach came to live with him and on same tract of land. Beach talked to him about getting Mr. Bradshaw's property and Carlton advised a deed of gift. "I moved William Beech from Lincoln County to this neighborhood in my waggon and he had little property not over forty or fifty dollars in value. Saw William Bradshaw's wife put arms about her husband kiss and etc, in public places."

At Rev. William Dodson's where they sat down to dinner, Mrs. Bradshaw directed the plate before Mr. Bradshaw be taken away and said they had already eat together off of one plate.

Elizabeth Carlton age 59 sworn, Benjamin Beech age 51 deposed "I am the eldest brother of William Beech. We bread up and in same family until he was sixteen or seventeen years old except one or two years. Lived near him when he was married. For last three or four years before he moved from neighborhood. William Beach had six or seven children.

Character witnesses. Overton County, Tennessee. 11 Jany 1821. Depositions of Nancy Hinds age 35 years; Polly Latham age 21 years; John S. Williams age 34 years; Joseph Evans age 26 years; Levy Hinds age 46 years; Nancy Hinds 35 years; Jany Cilcock age 22 years; Peggy Storie age 17 years; Solomon Silcock age 28 years; John Van hooser age 56 years; Joshua Storie age 54 years; Squre Angelea age 22 years; Robert Storie age 36 years; John S. Williams age 62 years; Robert Storie age 36 years; All sworn in Overton County at house of Joshua Storie, Jan. 21, 1822.

Nancy Hinds asked or said something about the Elizabeth Bradshaw at the hearing. Adam Huntsman was the defendant's council.

Others who testified, Joseph Evans age 36 years; William Grimsley age 59 years. He was pastor of the church. Said William Beach was a member of the Baptist order. They were members of the same church. Isaac Denton age 54 years, Member of same church and he had the care of the church; Philip Smith, age 52 a member of the same church; Thomas Wood age 43; Thomas Scott age 66 years; Thomas Scott stated that he knew him speaking of Bradshaw, about thirty years and knew him when they lived in Burke County, North Carolina. They were members of the same church in North Carolina and in Overton County, Tennessee.

Joseph Poore age 48 years made a deposition. Others who made depositions were Margery Poore age 43 years; Nelly Garrott age 39 years (knew Bradshaw about two years); Sally V. Hooser age 17 years; Susan Beach age 17 years; James Cowan age 57 years; John V. Hooser age 57 years (father of Sally above); John S. Williams age 34 years; P. M. Miller was the attorney for the defendant.

John McIver of Overton County, in his deposition stated that he first knew Mr. Bradshaw about September 1816. He was about seven years old. Mr. William Fleming made a deposition in the town of Monroe 1820.

Henry Reagan age 58 years; Wm. Atkinson age 31 years; Benjamin Totten age 42 years; George Armstrong age 33 years; William Fleming age 32 years, and Conrac Pile age 54 years, all gave depositions.

Henry Reagan age 58 years, Joseph Evans age 36 years; Rachel West age 26 years (was granddaughter of Mr. Bradshaw in N. C.); Samuel Odle age 24 years; Absalom Garrett age 48 years; Nancy Vanhooser age 45 years; Henry Reagan age 26 in January 1822; Benjamin Pooer was aged 49 years; Joseph Dunkin; Jane Johnston. Seems most of these were people who resided in Overton County, Tennessee. Davidson Jones age 51 years. Joshua Storey was 53 years of age. Joseph Duncan mentioned.

Fentress County, Deed Book D, page 638. The will of Squire Angle names: William Angle; Louisa Angle; Martha Angle; Polly Angle; Martin Angle; Alexander Angle; Elizabeth Angle; Margaret Angle. Widow, Polly Angle. Also, Ambrose Angle; Alfred Angle; Allen Angle; Shadrack Garrett; Thomas Garrett; and John Buck.

Deed Book D, page 779. John V. (or H ?) Richardson, Will in Fentress County, names: Stockley D. H. Richardson; Abbeville Richardson; Robert Richardson; Eveline Richardson; Henry H. Richardson; William H. Richardson; Jeffrey H. Richardson; Robert H. Richardson and John M. Richardson.

INDEX

www.ingramcontent.com/pod-product-compliance
Lightning Source LLC
Chambersburg PA
CBHW072207270326
41930CB00011B/2558
* 9 7 8 0 8 0 6 3 0 8 4 1 8 *